# The Wrecking of the Orion

## Jayne Baldwin

Published by Second Sands Publications 2020
an imprint of Foggie Toddle Books,
18 North Main Street,
Wigtown.
DG8 9HL

ISBN 9780992657628

Cover images from *The Illustrated London News June 29th 1850*

# Contents

*The Steam Ship Orion – illustration from The Wreck of the Orion
by Rev Joseph Clarke published 1851*

Then rose from sea to sky, the wild farewell –
Then shrieked the timid, and stood still the brave –
Then some leap'd overboard with dreadful yell,
As eager to anticipate their grave.

**Excerpt from The Shipwreck by Lord Byron**

# Chapter One

*"She almost seemed proud of her own powers, of her own length and breadth, and especially of the large and cheerful assemblage of passengers who she bore away."*

When Captain Alexander McNeill, the fifth Laird of Colonsay, carried his six-year-old daughter, Hester Mary, onto the deck of the splendid paddle steamer, the Orion, he would have felt something of a sense of relief. Along with his wife, his two teenage sons and his elder daughter, the family had endured a lengthy journey cooped up in coaches and railway carriages all the way from London to the bustling port of Liverpool. Further voyages lay ahead before they would finally reach their home on the tiny Hebridean island of Jura, where they would spend the summer. For the Scott family who had just disembarked from the ship the Europa after travelling from their home in Montreal across the Atlantic, there was a feeling of almost being there. After the strains of a lengthy ocean voyage there was just the safe and swift last leg of their journey ahead to visit family in Glasgow. John and Betsy Splatt and their four adult daughters were thinking of this overnight sailing as something of a pleasure trip before joining the ship that would take them on a long and dangerous voyage to Australia. Their older children had spent years persuading them to join them in Melbourne where they had prospered. Finally, after a lifetime of working the land, John had sold his farm in Devon and with their lifesavings stitched into Betsy's dress they were looking ahead to travelling to the other side of the world on the Admiral, sailing from Glasgow in a few days' time.

The Orion was the flagship of the fleet operated by the well-established Glasgow and Liverpool Steamship Company and she held the record for being the fastest of the vessels that regularly ran the sea route between these two powerhouse ports of Victorian Britain. The 17th of June 1850 was a beautiful summer's day; the forecast was good, and the ship was captained by an experienced man in charge of an equally experienced crew. The sailing was widely regarded as a safe one with little risk, the coast was well lit, and the ship soundly built. And yet, in the early hours of the following morning many of these men, women and children would meet their deaths within reach of land along with forty other passengers and crew. The McNeill boys would be orphaned, and John Splatt left a broken man. It was a tragedy that shook the nation not only due to the high death toll but because of the circumstances of the wrecking – so close to the small coastal village of Portpatrick in south west Scotland and in perfect weather with no hint of danger.

Liverpool's quaysides were a hive of activity, as usual, on that June afternoon, as the passengers for the three o'clock sailing to Glasgow waited for the signal for them to step aboard the paddle steamer. The Orion was the vessel of choice for anyone wishing to travel to Glasgow; much admired for speed, style and the elegance and extent of her cabin and saloon accommodation. Operated by the ship owners G & J Burns and described by the company as "perfect", the 899-ton iron steamer had been built in Greenock by Messrs Caird & Co and launched from their yard, number 14, on the 19th December 1846. She had a 200 feet long keel, 210 ft 6 in length in all, 18 ft 6 in depth of hold, she was 28 feet across the beam and had a more than 44 feet high main mast. The two other masts were in proportion to the main mast, though none were ever used during a sailing, and the two paddles on either side of the ship were powered by a two-cylinder side lever 460 horse power engine which gave a top speed of 14 knots (approximately 16 miles per hour). Although it was a passenger vessel, the Orion also had room for 20 tons of general cargo in the hold and during the afternoon travellers waited while she was loaded with eight tons of sheet iron, iron rods, bags of iron nails and some machinery. The loading of the cargo came under the direction of Daniel McKellar, the shipping clerk at Liverpool for the Steamship company, rather than the Orion's captain.

The sailing was fully booked with 115 cabin class passengers on board whose accommodation was divided between the fore and main of the ship. Many more were travelling steerage, which meant finding a seat where they could, and which for some would mean making the voyage on deck, huddling at night in sheltered spots, by the warmth of the funnel or in a nook by the lifeboats. One traveller was 39-year-old Reverend Joseph Clarke who would later publish a book about his experiences on the Orion. He wrote: "The vessel had been advertised, to leave the Clarence Dock at three pm. In order therefore to reach it without bustle I engaged a cab at about a quarter past two." The reverend had first gone for lunch at a place called Fisks and although he arrived at the dock in time to go on board, find his berth and make a complaint about it to the steward who promised to try and change it once everyone had arrived, he then discovered that he had left his shawl at the restaurant and had to call another cab to retrieve it. On returning to the dock he found that the cab driver had dropped him at the wrong side for the Orion and he urgently had to make his way through the crowds and paraphernalia of a busy quayside to return to the ship. "The steam appeared to be getting more and more 'up' as they say and making more and more noise – the passengers on board too were evidently bidding adieu to their friends and at length a call was made to those on the pier to go to the ropes. It was an exciting moment. I shouted stop...stop with no little alarm."

Mr Clarke, who was making a much anticipated return trip to the Highlands, managed to reach the iron bridge connecting the pier to the ship before it closed and made it on board just in time, joining his fellow passengers who numbered more than 150, many lining the rails to wave and call their final farewells. Luckily, or perhaps unluckily, for the reverend, the departure of the Orion had been slightly delayed while three other ships negotiated the Mersey on their way into dock and it was well past four o'clock before the paddle steamer finally began its journey towards the Irish Sea. Mr Clarke commented: "As soon as she made her safe escape through the mouth of the dock and reached the open Mersey – where her immense engines could move freely – then she almost seemed proud of her own powers, of her own length and breadth, and especially of the large and cheerful assemblage of passengers who she bore away. With apparently so much ease. It was indeed a pleasing sight, and the fine afternoon conduced much to render it so; for all could be on deck, and lounge or read, converse or walk about, just as they felt disposed."

The Orion was packed to the gunnels. The cabins were all fully booked, and the Rev Clarke was not the only one to hurry onto the vessel at the last moment. Many members of the clergy were heading north from Yorkshire and Lancashire for a conference and for the Rev. George Thomson and his wife there was an eleventh-hour change of mind about their arrangements. They had been due to travel to Scotland by rail but finding that the Orion was scheduled to sail that afternoon, with a fair forecast, they decided to journey by sea instead: "it being the finest vessel of the fleet and to gratify Mrs Thomson's wish to witness a voyage from Liverpool," the minister later wrote. The prospect of a fifteen-hour sailing on a warm sunny summer day must have seemed a far more attractive prospect than rattling along in an enclosed rail carriage. The couple were among a number who joined the vessel shortly before sailing, and though this was not unusual, there were too many for the steward to keep account of. Steerage passengers normally numbered between forty and sixty, the second steward John McHaffie would later admit that he did not know how many people had come on board, there were too many arriving too quickly to make a list.

When the Reverend Clarke eventually found a steward - the crew included a principal, three further stewards and a stewardess - he was informed that the voyage was heavily overbooked and there were more passengers looking for accommodation than there were cabins available. Many would be seeking rest on the couches and sofas in the saloon areas. Given this information the clergyman decided to take his belongings to the original berth he had complained about realising he was lucky to have it, and which he later described in his book: "The fore cabin might be said to be divided into two compartments by the staircase at the foot of which were folding doors opening into those compartments. The one I was to sleep in contained only six berths, viz, two on each of the three sides, the doorway being on the fourth. And as there was only the length of about eighteen inches behind the door for everything in the shape of dress etc and three or four carpet bags had already been heaped upon it, there was of course no room for anything else in the place, except on top of the berths."

In 1850 the Orion was still being advertised as The Glasgow and Liverpool Steamship Company's 'new' paddle-steamer, its captain, Thomas Henderson, also named in the frequent newspaper advertisements. There were regular sailings, three round trips every fortnight and the notice in the Liverpool Standard and General Commercial Advertiser on Tuesday the 18th June (the day the Orion was wrecked) announced that the ship would be sailing on the following Tuesday at half past one o'clock calling, weather permitting, at Ramsay Bay on the Isle of Man to land and receive passengers. Fares were ten shillings for a cabin with a steward's fee of two shillings and steerage passengers paid five shillings. Passengers were requested to take charge of their own luggage as the ship was not responsible in any way for its safety. Enquiries and bookings to T Martin, Burns & Co, 7 Water Street, Liverpool.

Shipping magnates, George and James Burns were two of four sons, a third was a passenger on the Orion's fateful voyage, born to the Rev. Dr John Burns and his wife Elizabeth. They established their first shipping company in 1824 running a passenger steamer service between Glasgow and Ayr before joining forces with a businessman called Hugh Mathie to start a small shipping line with six sailing vessels trading between Glasgow and Liverpool. In 1830 they began working with two Liverpool based Scots, David, and Charles MacIver to create the Glasgow Steam Packet Company with ships trading between Glasgow, Liverpool, Belfast and Londonderry. The Liverpool to Glasgow steamship route, or station as it was often called, had been established by shipping companies also early as 1819 with sailings calling at Douglas on the Isle of Man and Portpatrick.

At the Scottish port passengers and goods would be taken off by small boat and ferried to the village. The twice weekly sailings setting out from Greenock on Tuesdays and Fridays, relied as much on their sails as their engines and took 22 hours to make the voyage. It was not many years before the steamers no longer called at Portpatrick due to the insufficient depth of water at the harbour, and instead, in either direction, passed at night. Any travellers wishing to join the ship would have to carry out a somewhat alarming procedure. They would gather in one of the village taverns and then around midnight they would take a smouldering peat from the fire and row out to wait for the passing steamer. As it came into view, they would wave the peat in the air allowing it to burst into flames and alert the ship's crew of their desire to be picked up.

The name of George Burns was already known in this port on the Rhins of south west Scotland, as he had played a small part in its economic demise. Portpatrick had once held a key role in travel and communication not only between mainland Scotland and Ireland but also between that country and England and Wales – even before the Union. The short 21-mile crossing between Portpatrick and Donaghadee had been used for centuries by travellers and the mail until the middle of the 19th century. The improvement of the rail link between London and Holyhead in 1848 led to all mail from London being routed through the Welsh port and transported to Dublin. The Scottish mail continued to pass through Portpatrick until the following year when George Burns heard that the Post Office was considering offering the mail contract to the Ardrossan Steam Navigation Company – one of many rivals in the highly competitive steam ship business. Burns offered to carry the mail for free on his ships and after the offer was accepted by the Admiralty and the Post Office, the new system began on the 9th of July 1849.

THE ILLUSTRATED LONDON NEWS.

THE "ORION" STEAMER.

*The Orion leaving Liverpool - Illustrated London News.*

Captain Hawes R.N., who had worked for the Admiralty and was the Government Superintendent of the Works at the Harbour of Portpatrick, was forced to sell off the stores and equipment that had been used for decades to maintain the harbour. He was allowed to keep one of the large boats and it was this boat, a year later, that would come to rescue some of the passengers from drowning after the wrecking of the Burns vessel – the Orion. After the disaster, the Marquis of Londonderry told the House of Lords that if the Post Office station had remained at Portpatrick, it would have been the means of saving lives that were lost, but a "narrow spirit of economy had been the occasion of that catastrophe."

# Chapter Two

*"She was almost shaving the rocks."*

As expected in such beautiful conditions, the Orion was making good time as she sailed at full speed along the coast of England and towards her destination – Glasgow, stopping at Greenock on the way. This vessel was the pride of the fleet, the doors were gilded, there were decorated panels, carved woodwork in the cabins and velvet sofas in the saloons. Spirits were high on deck amongst the passengers who were enjoying the warmth of the day and the bracing sea air. The Rev Clarke described the scene in his book The Wreck of the Orion A Tribute of Gratitude published initially in 1851: "Even now, I could fancy myself on board, pacing to and fro – wending my way among the crowds – or seated at the end of the 'companion' taking notice of all that was going on."

He enjoyed the spectacle, describing some of the people he passed as he strolled around, or watched from his seat. A little girl, three intellectual looking gentlemen, a young fair-haired man who was paying attention, possibly flirting, with four young women before taking the arm of the eldest and perambulating along the deck, discoursing in many subjects. Mr Clarke appears to have been happy to view the interactions of others saying that there was only one gentleman who he may have felt inclined to strike up a conversation with, he was "a short, stout, comely looking old gentleman, who, from his dress and appearance, might be taken for a clergyman or a doctor. His broad brimmed hat and gold headed cane led me to conjecture the former rather than the latter: and his evident affability towards all around convinced me of his kindness and good nature. At one time he was conversing pleasantly with ladies; at another with the gentlemen: now with one who seemed to be his daughter and now with the captain of the vessel, as if he took great interest in her progress."

The crowds who promenaded around the deck making the most of the fine weather and sea breezes reflected many walks of Victorian society from the great and the good, to those from humbler origins. The gentleman described by Mr Clarke was, he later learned, the brother of the ship's owners, which explained his familiarity with young Captain Henderson and interest in the way the journey was progressing. He was 76-year-old Dr John Burns, the eldest of the Burns brothers and a graduate of the University of Glasgow where he was the first Regius Professor of Surgery. A highly respected and learned man, he was the author of several student textbooks and was an international authority on midwifery amongst other medical subjects.

The four young women described could have been the daughters of John and Elizabeth Splatt who were on their way to join the ship that would take the family to Australia. For many years, the couple had resisted the arguments of their older son William to emigrate to the colony after he, and two other siblings had made a successful life there. After much persuasion John Splatt had finally agreed to make the long and hazardous journey with the rest of his family, selling the farm in Devon and carrying with them the 600 sovereigns that were their life savings.

The atmosphere on board had a cosmopolitan feel. Dinner had been served at three o'clock to cater for several passengers who had transferred directly from the Europa, a New York to Liverpool steamer that had arrived in the port earlier the same day. Others were returning home like one young woman who had sailed to Liverpool to wish a fond farewell to a brother in the Merchant Navy who was about to embark on his first voyage. Captain Alexander McNeill, the Laird of Colonsay, and his wife, Anne, and four children, daughters Cecil, 17, Hester Mary, six, and sons 19-year-old John and 15-year-old Alexander were on their way home to the tiny Hebridean island of Jura after collecting their eldest son from the East India Company Military Seminary at Addiscombe, Croydon. Retired banker John Roby, who was also an accomplished author and poet, was on his way to Edinburgh with his wife and daughter.

Stories were exchanged, new friendships formed as some stayed on deck and others retired to the saloons where they could rest, read newspapers and books, perhaps play cards with family or acquaintances. Tea was served at a quarter to eight with the saloon becoming so crowded on such a warm evening that the steward had to open the deck windows. Among the large number of women taking the journey were several who, though English, had just returned from America and were talking with each other about the scenery they had seen, the canals, steamers and the places and people they had left behind.

For Reverend Clarke, although the sea continued to be flat calm and it was a fine evening, as a rather private man he decided to retire to his berth at six o'clock, finding that someone else had actually preceded him and had already taken ownership of one of the berths. To the clergyman's greater surprise his cabin companion had decided to lie down on top of his bunk quite fully clothed. Following this lead, Mr Clarke decided to do the same and after finding enough room to kneel for a short prayer, he lay down using his jacket, overcoat and wrapper as coverings instead of using the blankets provided. But despite being pleased with the comfort of the berth, Mr Clarke was unable to rest due to many other passengers continuing to enjoy the delights of the company and the pleasant evening on the deck above him. "The constant pacing of footsteps overhead was an effectual barrier to all attempts to sleep. Tread, tread, again and again, so the monotonous sound continued for hours."

It had been late before many cabin passengers decided to retire. According to the Chelmsford Chronicle, "Up until 11 o'clock the night was spent in the most agreeable and cheerful manner by all, at which hour the greater number in the cabins retired to sleep." One of the people enjoying the evening was a Stirling man, Adam Forbes, later described by the Reformers Gazette as "an intelligent steerage passenger". It was such a beautiful evening, no wind, the sea calm and smooth as glass, that it wasn't until going up to 10 o'clock that Mr Forbes decided to go below to the steerage saloon, an area below the quarter-deck at the stern of the ship, behind the engine rooms. Below he found everyone was "cheerful, with singing and merriment going on." In the cabin class deck most of the 'ladies' had retired at around 10 o'clock leaving just a few chatting and reading amongst the gentlemen who were engaged in conversation, taking refreshment for the night or taking part in games such as chess, backgammon and draughts.

In Mr Clarke's cabin, to the fore of the ship, each occupant of the remaining four berths slowly found their way to bed, giving the reverend hope that he would finally get to sleep, only to be disturbed again by the steward who arrived in the cabin to light the oil lamp which, much to his annoyance, happened to be set onto the wall by his berth. Despite his protests the steward insisted the lamp had to be fitted there and left it blazing brightly near the minister's head. Finally, the pacing on deck began to fade away, the rhythmical beat of the engine and swish of the paddles replacing the sound of footsteps.

Mr Clarke wrote: "I could tell by the smooth and regular motion of the vessel, that the night was as calm as the day had been. Sometimes I wondered whereabouts we were." On deck the first watch had been taken by George Langlands, a 26-year-old mariner from Argyll who had been the Orion's first mate since the preceding September. He had joined the ship just a month after Thomas Henderson had been appointed captain, replacing Captain Hugh Main who had been in command since she was launched. The sailing was proceeding as usual. The log of the Orion from a run earlier in June illustrates the travel times expected from the paddle steamer.

*Commenced 1.50pm*
*Sailed from Liverpool. Wind NW*
*Light at 8.45pm Point of Ayre [Isle of Man]*
*Mull of Galloway 10.15pm*
*Portpatrick 11.40pm*
*Sunday 2nd June*
*Light winds rain west.*
*Corsewall 12.40am*
*Ailsa 2.15am*
*Pladda 3.15am*
*Cumbrae 4.35am*
*Arrived Greenock 6.05am*
*Glasgow 9.10am Day calm and sultry.*

On the 17th of June the Orion finally left Liverpool at 4.20pm and the ship passed the Point of Ayre at 10.25pm. One traveller later reported that the "weather had been so beautiful and calm that in passing the Isle of Man at about 10 o'clock, the atmosphere was clear enough to enable passengers to notice a windmill [on the island], and to distinguish the roofs of the houses." The Rev George Thomson was chatting with some of the American passengers on deck as the Orion passed the Point of Ayre before deciding to retire at about 11 o'clock, his wife having taken to her berth some time before due to feeling seasick. The minister decided to take a stroll below deck on his way to the cabin and later described the scene: "I took a walk up the centre of the saloon to see the groups that still lingered there. I found one party playing chess, another draughts, and another a game of whist. On the other table three or four small groups were enjoying a glass of toddy but all were quiet, pleasant and happy."

The Scottish coast was sighted shortly before midnight just as the first mate's watch was ending. They were passing the Mull of Galloway, the most southerly point in Scotland at the bottom of the area known as the Rhins, with the land clearly visible, though there was a very slight fog. Captain Henderson had been on deck, supervising the changeover from his first mate to the second mate, John Williams, a knowledgeable officer from Liverpool. The 54-year-old was very familiar with this voyage having sailed the route for many years before joining the Orion eleven months before.

Although all experienced seamen, the officers had all been with the Orion for less than a year, but with three round trips a fortnight they had plenty of practise at negotiating the tides and currents around this stretch of the UK's coastline. The seaman who had the helm from 10 o'clock until the change of watch at midnight, was David Walker of Glasgow who had been with the Orion for eighteen months; he believed the vessel was unusually close to the Mull. The author of The Loss of the Steamer Orion, Gordon Bodey wrote in his article published in the bulletin of the Liverpool Nautical Research Society: "Although the depth of water there is adequate his [Walker's] concern may have been due to knowing the danger presented by the very strong tidal race off the point; present-day advice is to give the point a three-mile offing."

This concern was shared by Donald McKinnon, a working seaman returning to Glasgow as a steerage passenger having piloted the wooden paddle steamer, the Commodore, from Fort William as far as the Mull of Kintyre, before traveling on with the ship to Liverpool. He was on the foredeck as the Orion passed the Mull of Galloway and later said that she was "almost shaving the rocks". Walker was on deck along with the captain, the first mate, George Williams, who had piloted the vessel along the Mersey, together with seamen James Donaldson, John Kerr and the ship's carpenter Andrew Walker, who had only joined the crew two weeks before. Two were acting as look-outs on the paddle bridge, which connected the two paddle boxes, but there was no one on the bows, though on the Orion the bridge was higher than on most other steamers giving good views forwards.

Walker was relieved at the helm by John Kelly and after staying for about five minutes he left the deck as the ship passed by Dunman Head, between the Mull and Portpatrick. But before he went below to sleep, he talked to George Williams about how close to land they were. When Kelly took over the wheel, he also felt concern at just how close the Orion was to the coast; he had served on the route for four years, twenty months with Captain Main before Captain Henderson took over command. In his experience he had never seen them passing so close to shore. Although the second watch was traditionally known as the captain's watch, ship owners did not specify that the commander was on deck, it was normally delegated to the second mate following instructions from his senior officer. Captain Henderson was observed looking at the ship's two compasses and then speaking with the second mate John Williams who subsequently gave a series of orders that would take them even further in towards land.

At Dunman Head, Kelly had been given a course of NW½W to steer, taking the Orion past Crammag Head about a mile farther on. Donald McKinnon, now standing in the bow, thought the vessel was in danger of striking the outlying rocks near the headland and yet the course was still progressively brought round to N½W. By this time Captain Henderson had gone below to his cabin to rest. In his berth, the Reverend Clarke had finally been lulled by the steady rhythm of the paddles and the regular beat of the engines into a light sleep: "A feeling of sleepiness came over me – a kind of dozing sleepiness

– till the discomfort of lying so long in boots obliged me to push them off; when lying down again I hoped to doze away more pleasantly the remainder of the night."

Steerage passenger Adam Forbes decided to take another stroll on the deck at around 1 am. It was a clear night with daylight faintly breaking to the east. He saw some women and children lying sleeping near the funnel and in other sheltered places on deck, though the air was not cold. Mr Forbes saw the second mate, the steersman, and a man at look-out walking the gangway. Noticing that the ship was now considerably closer to shore, after twenty minutes he again returned below in the company of two other steerage passengers. Now many were lying asleep while others continued with their stories and songs. Taking a seat on the starboard side facing land, he rested back listening to the background hum of voices talking, singing, joke telling and laughing. After an afternoon and evening filled with the light-hearted atmosphere of the regular paddle steamer outings, popular in the period, the passengers had finally settled into slumber or whispered conversations. In adjoining berths numbers 80 and 81, Hugh and George Miller, two brothers from Alloway Place, Ayr, slept soundly, while in a separate compartment Elizabeth Colquhoun and her cousin Mary Houston finally closed their eyes after an exhausting afternoon keeping watch on the latter's two very young children.

The Orion was making good time. Sailing at full steam the ship was on target to make the passage in its usual 15 or 16 hours, John Kelly would later explain, if they reached Greenock by 8 o'clock. The aim was to "run with the tide" to Glasgow, but an hour after that and the opportunity would be lost, the change of tide slightly slowing the Orion's speed. It was at around 1.30am when the helmsman John Kelly heard the look-out Wilson, who was employed as the Clyde pilot, shout out from the gangway that there was a "light on the starboard bow." Moments later he walked back to where the second mate was standing to say "John, do you see no land there?" to which Williams replied "Yes" but that was his only comment. There was no change in course and Kelly next heard a look-out call that there was a vessel on the port bow with no light. As they passed near Dunskey, where the ruins of an ancient castle stand on a cliff top, Kelly caught sight of Portpatrick lighthouse; Williams told him to keep "starboard a little – keep her north by west." There was no change of speed and the Orion sailed on at her full 14 knots. Suddenly there was a terrified shout from Duncan Campbell on look-out: "Hard starboard" followed by "land right ahead!" Williams had been standing by the mizzen-rigging and now ran towards the aft skylight, near where the captain's cabin lay below, and then on to help Kelly at the helm, both men hauling at the wheel turning it hard a starboard – but it was too late. The Orion, the pride of the fleet, travelling at full speed, hit rocks with the shuddering scream of metal being ripped apart by stone.

# Chapter Three

*"Get out the boats for she won't live five minutes."*

Fisherman David Adair was still awake in the early hours of the 18th June, baiting lines in an upstairs room of his home on North Crescent, opposite the end of the pier, when he saw the Orion come into view. It was a familiar sight, steamers passed Portpatrick regularly on their journeys north and south but the 23-year-old had never seen a ship sailing so close to shore and he later described the distance as about a "gunshot away" from where he was. Alarmed, he immediately ran out of the house heading for Ward Bay, to the north of the village – believing that from her speed and course she would be dangerously near the rocks there.

His neighbour John Okey was lying in bed reading and heard the familiar sound of the paddle steamer. He went up to his garret window to watch her pass by; he could see her bright lights and the speed she was travelling. He thought from her proximity to the village she was heading into the harbour, she was so close. When she did not, he decided to dress quickly fearing, like his neighbour, that she was taking a dangerous course but as he turned away from the window, he heard the crash – a long unmistakable sound. Along the crescent David Armstrong, a 54-year-old fisherman, was also still awake in the early hours as he was unwell and had been pacing restlessly around his room. His house was opposite the mouth of the harbour and he watched the Orion pass the south pier. "I think if I'd been on the pier, I could have pitched a pebble stone on her" he would later say. He too was convinced she was heading into the small harbour even though there was not the depth of water or length of pier to accommodate her. As he sat back down on his bed, he heard his daughter call to him that the steamer "was ashore."

Faintly dozing in his seat in steerage, Adam Forbes heard the crash like "a peal of thunder. I thought something had gone wrong with the engine, it was like a heavy fall of machinery." In his berth the Reverend Clarke had been sleeping for about half an hour when he was woken again by a loud noise, like a "tearing or rending" of the vessel. Looking over the side of his berth he saw that boots and clothes were already floating, with water gushing forcefully into the cabin. Jumping down he found himself knee deep in water even though only a few moments had passed. He hurried out towards the cabin stairs but turned back to collect his bag and what he thought was his coat.

In another cabin Elizabeth Colquhoun was sleeping along with her cousin Mary Houston, who was the wife of James Houston, a shipmaster from Port

Glasgow, and her children, James who was just a month short of his third birthday, and his younger sister Mary age two. When the two women woke the water was already filling the cabin and there was no time to dress. The Miller brothers were woken by a "hard bumping sound and shake" followed immediately by the torrent of water rushing into the cabin. Like the Reverend Clarke had discovered, they were quickly knee deep in seawater and they struggled to find the door as there was "great confusion." As they joined the throng of passengers in the confines of the cabin deck they found the stairs were "strewed with ladies shawls, gowns left in fearful struggle for precedence, ladies crying for husbands and brothers, husbands for wives and daughters, mothers for children and children for parents. Amid this painful excitement the hoarse voice of a sailor on deck proclaiming the awful truth 'get out the boats, for she won't live five minutes.'" (1)

Joseph Clarke wrote the following year of those first few moments after the Orion struck the rocks just yards north of Portpatrick. "The scene is still as vividly before me as it was then. There came, pouring up from the main cabin, men and women, just as they had risen from their beds, some half-dressed and many in their nightdresses only; all too much alarmed to care much about their appearances – running from one side of the vessel to the other – wringing their hands in silent dread – and then exclaiming 'she is going down', 'she is going down', 'what shall we do', 'Lord have mercy on us.' That the vessel was indeed sinking rapidly at her bows was quite clear to us all."

Adam Forbes was one of the last to get to the hatchway from the steerage saloon, and immediately went towards the bow of the ship – "the steam was going off through the steam pipe making a fearful noise." He was astonished at the vessel's proximity to the land and felt that he could have thrown a stone at the rocks from where he was. The Orion was starting to tilt onto her side obliquely to the shore but was veering round with her head towards land and rapidly settling down at the bow. Another eyewitness, who referred to himself in newspaper reports as a 'seafaring' man, was sleeping on the port side in the foremost part of the ship when he was woken by a sudden shock and instantly got out of bed, waking his friend and urging him to gather his belongings quickly as the water was rushing in "with great violence." On deck many of the passengers were in a state of near nudity, and shock. His first thought was to see how far land was away and he could distinctly see the breakers on the shore, less than a quarter of a mile distant, with Portpatrick lighthouse in plain sight. He knew there was no time to be lost.

On board were many children either travelling with their parents or other relatives. One of them was Harriet McKenzie Peughe, the 12-year-old daughter of the Episcopalian minister for Paisley, who was under the care of the stewardess, Mrs Blain. After the alarm was given, she proceeded to help the terrified girl to dress, and took her on deck, "the poor little child exclaiming, 'I know you will not leave me.'—'No, no, I never will,'" the woman was heard to answer.

The engines had come to an immediate halt at impact, one passenger saying there was not even one half turn further of the paddles. The fearful noise of the steam was caused by the immediate flooding of the engine room and the crucial advice of one passenger, a man connected with the railways, who urged one of the firemen to blow off the steam, the release preventing the boilers from bursting and causing the ship to explode. Mr Clarke was a witness: "The water, coming in contact with the fires and boilers, caused a terrific explosion. Both water and fire blew up with a tremendous noise. Many of us at once concluded that the vessel had ignited and would, in a short time, be consumed in flames."

The speed at which the steamer was sinking was a shock to all, passengers, and crew – it would take less than 15 minutes from impact to the Orion being almost completely submerged in five fathoms of water. Just as more than fifty years later people would be astonished at the sinking of the famous liner The Titanic, the wrecking of the Orion would cause a similar reaction amongst the general public in the weeks after the disaster. She had been built for safety with watertight bulkheads divided into four or five compartments designed to protect the vessel from sinking should she run aground or hit rocks. Like the legendary ship more than half a century later, the Orion was thought to be unsinkable but shipbuilders had never imagined that she would be sailed full throttle so close to land. The rock she hit had ripped through several of those supposedly watertight compartments and she was sinking rapidly.

Some people, though, crucially including the captain, initially believed that they were in no real danger. It was not that unusual for steamers to hit sandbanks and at first there were many who thought that the ship had simply run aground, and they would need to allow for the tide to move them off; either that, or given the closeness of the coast, they would simply wait for low tide and walk to safety. But there were others who were very afraid and in a panic, and when he emerged from his cabin Captain Thomas Henderson was seen to stand on the engine house in his shirt and drawers attempting to calm the increasingly vocal throng of people, now rushing on to the deck. He was clearly heard shouting to all to "keep calm" – reassuring them that that they were not in danger and threatening to "cut the hand off" the first man to touch the lifeboats.

He asked the women to compose themselves, assuring them that there was no need for alarm, but this was questioned by one woman who just been to the cabin to urge her fellow female passengers to dress quickly as she had seen that the ship was already going down at the bow. George Thomson would later recall the captain saying that "if they all stuck to the ship there would be no danger" and he went below to advise the women of this situation but as the water rose and vessel lurched their panic was renewed.

The lack of leadership from any of the officers, and the captain's behaviour would be commented on by many of the survivors. William Anderson, an accountant from Glasgow, said: "I think there was a gross and culpable carelessness shown, first in striking the rock and next in getting the boats let down. The crew seemed paralysed and as helpless as any passengers." Similarly, a Mr Deuchars told the Liverpool Times that he "did not see the captain, the mate or the engineer on deck, nor did I see the crew exerting themselves in saving the people as much as they ought to have done."

The following year Reverend Clarke echoed his words: "No one could be seen exercising anything like authority. The wheel was abandoned and the crew I know not where. We seemed to be left entirely to ourselves. 'Where is the captain?' I shouted. In two or three minutes afterwards, he was in the midst of us – and immediately getting up on the end of the skylight, urged us not to leave the vessel with the assurance that 'she would not go down.'" After this the clergyman claimed that he neither saw nor heard the captain give any direction or exert himself in any way to save those who were in his care.

Along with the rest of the distressed crowd, he ran here and there desperate for experienced guidance as to what they should do. But confusion reigned. In the account given to The Scotsman by the Miller brothers they said that the "consternation was indescribable. Amid boisterous orders and rude efforts of the more active and the exclamation and grief of the helpless, attempts were made to clear the boats of their entanglements."

The Orion had four lifeboats, two on the quarter deck, one on each side, and one behind each paddle box. All hung on davits with three supporting chocks underneath, lashed with canvas covers, which were laced under the keel and on top of that Captain Henderson had instructed the new carpenter to fashion spray screens and bolt them to the deck. As the ship lurched again there was a terrible panic to get into the lifeboat on the starboard side, which was now nearer the water, the ship sinking broadside to starboard with the bows going down first. A crowd of cabin and steerage passengers, many of them women along with two or three crew were surging round the boat – the mariners making no organised effort to hold the people back according to witnesses.

Reverend Clarke heard the knocking of hammers near the paddle box on the larboard side, then the name for port, and went to see the strenuous efforts being made to try to release the boat from its supports and elaborate coverings. The intense stress of the situation was exacerbated by not only the complication of the covers, and the chocks but the tackle mechanism also seemed to be stuck. Eventually, with difficulty, the first of the boats crammed with people including Adam Forbes and an Alloa man, John Archibald with his young son William, was being lowered when the stern rope stuck fast while the bow rope still ran on, throwing most of the occupants into the water.

"The boat was hanging almost perpendicular, the bow partly in the sea, a quarter of the boat underwater. I was thrown into the sea but managed to get hold of the boat again and held fast to one of the seats. One or two people were hanging from the seats, several were in the water, some clinging, others sinking to rise no more. There was a cry from the ship above to cut the stern rope, which someone did. The boat fell plunging down, capsizing, and floating keel up. With others I went underwater again but rose up and I got hold of the keel," Adam Forbes later recalled.

Alerted by cries of "the boat is swamped," "they are drowning", Reverend Clarke witnessed Mr Forbes and others clinging to the first lifeboat. "With the eager and anxious hope of being saved too many had crowded into that first boat or else it had been lowered from the vessel unskilfully. And being capsized, all, apart from the two or three clinging to the keel were plunging – sinking – drowning around it. A number of us immediately seized hold of one of the ropes by which the boat had been lowered and pulled and pulled but – though we pulled the ropes – they brought not with them either boat or living being. O dreadful sight, some had sunk to rise no more – and others were giving the last faint movement of hands and head."

One of the crew, James Stewart, who had been on watch threw one of the cork fenders down to the people from the swamped boat who were desperately thrashing in the sea. These fenders were placed in various parts of the ship and were used to absorb the energy of the Orion when berthing at a jetty or quayside. John Archibald and his son had been pitched into the sea as the lifeboat fell, and had found themselves struggling in the water, pulled down by other panicking passengers grabbing onto their arms. John managed to make his way back to the surface and with his son grabbed hold of the fender, along with two other men and waited for rescue.

As the ship lurched again, the increasingly sloping deck poured the sliding passengers towards the sea, amongst them were Elizabeth Colquhoun and her cousin, Mary Houston with the two children. Elizabeth managed to grasp one rope but lost hold and was under the water for some time before managing to resurface and grab hold of another. As she had rushed up onto the deck, she had been clutching her cousin's little boy in her arms but lost hold as they were all plunged into the sea.

Adam Forbes, aware of how close the coast was, considered swimming as the surface of the water was still quite smooth but "so many women and children were floating and struggling" that he was afraid to "strike out." He did make one attempt but was immediately caught by both arms and, after freeing himself from the other person's urgent grip, struggled with difficulty back again to the upturned boat. He witnessed how rapidly the steamer was going down and helplessly watched as a great number of people launched themselves from the ship.

Ropes were thrown over from the deck and some lowered themselves down. He managed to get hold of one woman and two men, all holding on to him and the rope to which he was clinging. They all then saw one of the lifeboats going past with only 15 people within it. "We screamed and shouted to take us off, it could have held 20 to 30 people, but the people in it paid no attention and made for shore. There were two or three firemen belonging to the ship in it," he would later tell reporters.

The helmsman, John Kelly, was also in this larboard boat that had been safely lowered into the water. When the ship hit the rock, he had immediately run to the lifeboat and with passengers, including commercial traveller John Cameron, several firemen and engineers, worked to get it lowered, cutting the lacing with his knife that strapped the cover over the top. Cameron and Kelly had each hold of a rope but as they got the boat level with the bulwarks the others all scrambled in. Cameron then jumped in, still holding the rope and when the boat reached the water Kelly swung down. But they then discovered there were neither oars nor any sign of the bung that should have been either loose or stored in the bottom of the boat along with a rudder, mast, and tiller. The boat was filling with water and over the side of the rail another seaman called to Kelly to go to the aid of the starboard boat that had capsized. Kelly shouted back that he had no oars and although some were thrown down to him, by passenger Thomas Kidston, it was not the number needed for each boat.

There was still no sign of the bung and one of the passengers, a sailor from Liverpool, made a makeshift solution by stuffing his handkerchief into the hole. There were only fifteen or twenty people in the boat, including the two Miller brothers from Ayr, and as they finally hauled away round the stern they could see the other boat had been swamped and people were floating in the water. Some of those on board felt they should try to rescue them but others, given the amount of water coming in, feared it would lead to them all being drowned even though the lifeboats were designed to take many more.

Instead they headed for shore believing it was best to rectify the problem and then return to render assistance, many of the men on board having to continually bail the water out with their hats. Mr Clarke saw the larboard lifeboat and how few 'ladies' were on board, noticing the number of men and crew "those who ought to have remained to the last and exerted themselves to the very utmost, to save and send off passengers; but who, like the captain, seemed to consider it the best part of valour to take care of themselves."

In 1850 it was not standard practice to consider women and children first in times of crisis. Although one would imagine that etiquette or social morals during this period would have seen precedence given to those less able to save themselves, it wasn't until two years later that the idea of "women and children first" came into practice due to another disaster, this time with a huge loss of life off the coast of South Africa. What is now known as the Birkenhead Drill came from the paddle steamship of that name which was carrying 634 troops and their families destined for the Frontier War. In similar circumstances to the Orion, HMS Birkenhead hit rocks, in this case uncharted, in a flat calm sea in the early hours of the morning. Lifeboats were lowered, encountering similar difficulties to those on the Orion, and the women and children were rowed to safety. The commanding officer drew his sword and told his men to stand fast, fearing that any of them swimming for their lives would swamp the lifeboats in their desperation to be saved. Instead the soldiers stood bravely on the deck as the ship slipped beneath the waves – only 193 survived.

On the Orion, for those who had not fallen or chosen to take their chances in the water there was only the prospect of holding on to the rising stern with the deck now at an increasingly desperate angle. One of these was the Glasgow accountant, William Anderson: "It would be vain to attempt depicting the terror, consternation and agony of those who now occupied the small portion of the quarter deck still above the water. To flee to the rigging was now their only hope of escape from a watery grave and this was generally resorted to in desperation as the broad blue waters rose around them in portentous silence, threatening every moment to engulf them." He managed to hold on to a rope fastened to a mast after being "plunged into the mighty deep when the last part of the quarter deck sank."

Another clinging desperately to the deck was Reverend Clarke: "While many were thus crowded on the lower starboard side, and obliged at last to cast themselves into the water – on bits of wood – planks – or spars – or whatever was nigh at hand – I had placed myself like several others on the upper bulwarks near the stern: where discovering a man hanging by a rope (which proves how perpendicular to the water the deck had become) I succeeded in drawing him up to the same place. On his left was seated and clinging to one of the davits a young girl having no covering over her shoulders – being evidently just as she had risen from her bed – and to all appearance waiting as calmly and quietly what was to follow"

The speed with which the Orion sank meant that by the time the fishing boats arrived from the village, the only parts of the vessel remaining were the masts and the funnel. From the rigging Captain Henderson was shouting orders and directing the rescuers to where people were floundering in the sea. There were those, who were able, who attempted to swim – they were mainly men and boys – though the ability to swim was no guarantee that they would make it to land. A stout gentleman from America was later reported to have thrown himself into the sea and made it to shore. One swimmer had seen a child floating nearby as a boat passed and seizing the infant managed to jerk the child in amongst the people on board.

Jonathon Settle, who was travelling with two friends, Robert Haslam and William Latham, had all slept on their bunks wearing their clothes and were sound asleep when the Orion was wrecked. Believing that his friends on the bottom bunks, had escaped from the cabin before him as the water was already higher than the beds, Mr Settle had plunged into the sea and set off for shore. Overcome by exhaustion he was picked up by one of the fishing boats and "remembered nothing until he found himself at Portpatrick." Although his friend Robert had been an "active man and an excellent swimmer" he had never made it out of the bunk. It came to light later that Robert Haslam had, in his pocket, a letter introducing him to Dr Burns and his reason for travelling to Scotland was to consult him about his health, having no idea that the eminent surgeon was also on the Orion.

Apart from the hindrance of their clothing, even nightdresses, women were far less likely to be able to swim, and without help either from men or floating wreckage, they stood little chance of surviving. Whilst sea bathing was regarded as a healthy pastime in the middle of the 19th century, most Victorian women in their billowing swimwear (gowns suitable to prevent indecent exposure of the body) would have been at best inexperienced swimmers. Most would have enjoyed immersion in the sea after being towed into the shallows in a bathing machine or lowered into the water by a woman employed to do that. However there were reports later that one woman, despite the terror felt by everyone around her, remembered that if a person lay on their back and moved their hands gently they could float for a long time – by doing this she was saved. (2)

There were small acts of bravery by women like a Miss Woolfield who tried to save her uncle's life by holding his ear whilst she held onto a rope. Sadly, her "slight grasp" as it was later described, soon yielded. But others were later reported to have acted with greater concern for their fellow passengers and made combined efforts to save each other. Though this was not the case with everyone, one man who had been attempting to save the lives of two women and his child with his chin propped on a plank to keep them all afloat, had the wood pulled away by another desperate passenger, and the child was lost. But for every selfish, frantic act there were many more where people acted with bravery and compassion.

The shock, the coldness of the water, and the physical toll of trying to deal with the ever-changing situation meant that exhaustion quickly overcame even the strongest. Many survivors later movingly recalled the gallantry of Captain Alexander McNeill who was seen clinging to a floating spar, guiding many to safety by his voice and his exertions, calming the "shrieking throng" who were floundering in the waters around him. One witness remembered, "his strength finally failed him and he was heard to cry 'for God's sake save yourselves, I have done all I can' and before rescue arrived the hero hearted captain was beyond the reach of succour." His two sons, John and Alexander did survive. Both boys, in their late teens, were strong swimmers, due to growing up in the Hebrides, and the eldest had been a cadet at the East India Company's Military Seminary at Addiscombe near Croydon.

Adam Forbes was eventually picked up by fisherman, David Adair in his 16-foot fishing boat, crewed by his neighbour John Okey. They were the first to reach the wreck and were faced with the most appalling scene. They had already collected a man from the stern of the ship and a woman from the water, but there were so many "grappling to get hold of the boat and everyone entreating to be saved in the most piteous manner." Mr Forbes was lucky, as he later admitted, for if he had needed to hold the rope for even five minutes more he would have been forced to let go as his arms and whole body were "benumbed with cold." The boat was so small that with eight people on board there was no room for anyone else, but as they rowed for the harbour, they passed four more local boats heading for the wreck. Mr Forbes looked back at the sinking ship and noticed that the sea had reached the funnel with just the quarter deck still above the water. "The screaming was heart-rending. There was still a great number on deck, some in the rigging and others holding on to pieces of wood and other articles."

The two fishermen managed to get everyone in the boat back to the pier and immediately Adair returned accompanied this time by a little boy and one of the firemen who had made it to safety in the larboard lifeboat whilst

Okey went to crew one of the other boats going out. The alarm had been raised throughout the small village and amongst the first to be alerted were Captain Edward Hawes and Mr Hannay who had immediately launched the Government harbour boat, manned by volunteer fishermen which saved 30 people.

Captain Hawes went out on the third boat while Mr Hannay remained to organise the further nine boats that went out all crewed by local men who had responded to the call from their beds. Patrick Horner, a labourer, had run down to the harbour from his home after hearing the cries of alarm from David Adair, David Armstrong, John Okey and other villagers. Armstrong, despite feeling unwell, ran to join one of the boats going out to the wreck. Horner arrived just as the larboard lifeboat was coming ashore with six or seven crew and a further 18 or 20 passengers, he estimated.

The boat was half full of water by the time it landed and those with enough energy began bailing it out with their shoes and hats. A proper plug was found to replace the handkerchief and Horner, along with two crew, started to push the boat back out to return to the wreck but after several paces he discovered it had something dragging from it; it was a rope fastened to the bottom of the boat with a davit suspended from it which had been snagging on rocks and preventing them relaunching.

The ship's cook, who had been in the first boat jumped out again on seeing so many people flailing in the water. Mr Jones, described in newspapers as a "man of colour" had been one of the first of the crew to work tirelessly to free up the lifeboats, and he had then leapt into the sea as he was an excellent swimmer and, in his own words, "could not keep the boat when so many fellow creatures were drowning before my eyes." He succeeded in saving several lives by pushing spars and boxes to those who were battling with the water.

Some people, mainly men, were managing to remain afloat as they waited for rescue by holding desperately on to floating wreckage. One man by chance found a footing on the starboard lifeboat which had sunk but remained suspended by the one rope about five feet below the surface of the sea. He managed to balance himself on the top of it, but the action of the tide made his footing increasingly precarious and, in the end, with increasing exhaustion he lost it. Thankfully, he spotted a floating piece of wood and managed to hold on to that until rescue.

A Frenchman, who many survivors would recall having a 'fine, long beard and moustache,' Monsieur G Lequiez clung to the rigging until he saw a plank and managing to climb on top, then paddled to safety. He had been travelling to Scotland to visit the Highlands with his companion Monsieur Jujuit after touring Switzerland. Mons Lequiez had wanted to travel by rail but his friend, a successful businessman who had lived in America for many years where he had owned four steamers, wanted to take the Orion. Both men survived.

One of the men on the shore boats on reaching what was left of the Orion knew the depth of water there and that even when she had gone down, the masts would remain above the surface and he called out to the terrified people who were left to "lay aloft"; those who understood him headed for the rigging. "Cries of every description were heard around, the weak and the tender implored help – more speedy help from the advancing boats, some prayed to God while others in the indescribable earnestness of agony for mercy, and others in the madness of despair cursed and blasphemed. Around were thickly strewn the bodies of the living and the dead, clinging to spars and the rigging. The vessel had sunk under about 15 feet of water carrying down both the dead and the living in her vortex and causing the calm sea to heave into high rolling waves."(3)

Reverend Clarke was one of those clinging to the upper bulkhead along with a man and young girl when the Orion went down: "We had scarcely time given to us to commit our souls into God's hand ere – with one terrible, instantaneous engulfment – the whole vessel sank down – carrying us along with her into the depths of the sea and causing at the same time (by the very rapidity of that downward movement) the air enclosed in the saloon to force off the top of the skylight, and so to throw us up again."

After being dragged down with the ship as she lurched beneath the waves, Reverend Clarke found himself pushed back to the surface with the air released from the lower decks – but there was no sign of the man or the young girl who had been holding on with him. He quickly found a box floating by but when he tried to grab it for support it turned repeatedly and soon exhausted what little strength he had. Being not much of a swimmer – "a few yards at best" – he had little chance of making the quarter mile to the shore. Just as he was making his peace with God, he spied a boat and with his last scrap of energy shouted: "'A boat, a boat' I called as loudly as I could. The men saw me not but heard the voice; and just as I felt myself turning round, perfectly powerless, their strong hand was upon me and dragged me in. There I lay at the bottom of the boat – conscious enough to hear what was said, but quite unable to move – with what feelings of thankfulness can easily be understood." As he lay there the body of a woman, who he believed to be dead, was also retrieved and thrown across his legs. Too exhausted to be able to extricate himself from under the body, he did revive enough to see the boatmen rowing and then standing to look for more bodies and shortly afterwards a man was rescued who was well enough to be able to sit on one of the benches. Moments later Reverend Clarke witnessed this man's rapturous reconciliation with his wife or sister when she was hauled into the boat alive. By then the boat was filling with water and the man then removed the woman's bonnet to join the fishermen in bailing as much out as they could as they headed for the quayside.

Mr Clarke then remembered little of how he was taken to safety at the home of one of the villagers. The Portpatrick fishermen continued to work to exhaustion trying to find as many people as possible. On the last run to the wreck there was a terrible quiet, a silence more dreadful than the screams and cries had been only minutes before. The last to be rescued from the wreck was Captain Henderson, who was reportedly standing on an iron crosstree of the main mast with his feet a yard from the surface of the sea, with his first mate George Langlands and one of the apprentice boys desperately holding on to the rigging of the main mast. George Thomson and his wife had been rescued in the same boat and were lying 'helpless' with exhaustion in the bottom. He would later recall: "As I lay in the stern I saw him [the captain] and another, who I think was one of the mates, sitting on the bench talking low and earnestly."

# Chapter Four

*"Then came the terrible swallowing up of everything and I saw him no more."*

When the cry went up that there was a steamer ashore, the people of Portpatrick immediately rallied. There had been wrecks before, of course, every coastal village had experienced the loss of vessels on their shores, but this was different. There was no storm, no high winds, it had been a perfectly lovely evening close to the summer solstice, so the sun barely went down. For no observable reason a paddle steamer that regularly passed along the coast had ploughed at full speed into rocks just yards north of the village, and even if she'd missed the rock, all agreed that due to the direction she was taking she would have crashed into the cliffs beyond. This was a poor village, since the loss of the Royal Mail and the ferry traffic to Ireland, people were reliant on fishing and labouring on local farms. Yet every household was prepared to help the survivors as they were brought to shore. Adam Forbes was struck by the sight of people running to the pier to help. "I shook terribly for several hours but they gave up their beds, provided warm drinks and other restoratives. I was treated with the greatest kindness," he told reporters later. But of the nine people taken to the same house, including two parents, two sons and three daughters only seven survived – two dying after arriving at apparent safety.

Children from households in the village were sent to the harbour to collect the traumatised survivors whilst the mothers stoked the ranges, gathered blankets and clothing and brought out the whisky which would be used not only to revive people but to rid pocket watches of sea water. "The hospitality of the people in Portpatrick was unbounded," the Reformers Gazette commented, "Bright fires were kindled and worn out survivors welcomed to a kindly hearth. Clothing was most liberally supplied and the medical gentleman, Dr Robertson after assisting in taking people off the wreck was indefatigable in his attention to all who stood in need of it." There were desperate scenes. A young man, who had rescued his child in one of the boats, found, on arriving at the pier that his wife had been left behind. He instantly gave his child to a fisherman's daughter, and went in search his wife; unable to find her among the survivors, he was seen to be going about almost frantic, having lost his wife, and not knowing where had left his child. Witnessing such suffering was distressing for everyone.

As the sun rose over the village the reality of the disaster became all too evident. On the pier lay the bodies of 25 people who just a few hours before had been enjoying, with high spirits, the delights of the voyage and the company of other passengers. A makeshift mortuary was quickly created in the village's former Custom House, owned by the Factor of the nearby Dunskey estate, a home Captain Hawes had only recently moved from. One of the empty rooms was prepared for the bodies and another for any belongings that had washed ashore or were being retrieved by the rescuers. There were soon more dead to add to that first total as many had died despite having made it to the shore alive including Captain McNeill's wife, Anne, and 17-year-old daughter, Cecil, who had been able to walk from the rescue boat up the steps of the harbour only a short time before. The body of the Captain's youngest child, six-year-old Hester Mary, would be washed ashore several days later at Dally Bay, not far from Corsewell lighthouse. The Orion's chief steward Alexander Graham, who had been with the company for 24 years, had gallantly repeatedly returned to cabins to retrieve blankets and clothing for the ladies, and managed to swim ashore. Sadly, he died of exhaustion soon after, despite the exertions of Dr Robertson. Although attempts were made to resuscitate many of those who had been brought ashore apparently lifeless, the main means of doing this at that time were based on the techniques established by the Society for the Recovery of the Drowned Dead, formed in Amsterdam in the late 18th century, later becoming the Royal Humane Society. These methods included warming the victim, ensuring the head was lower than the feet and applying pressure to the abdomen. (1) There were still many others from the more than 200 people on board, that were missing presumed dead.

The 12 boats that had gone out from the village saved the lives of 115 people and under the direction of Captain Hawes, the exhausted men returned to the wreck to bring in the bodies of the drowned and any luggage found floating. The captain advised them "not to let the stain of plunder come upon them" and to their great credit they obeyed him faithfully even though some of the dead were carrying large amounts of money, £200 was found on one man – a fortune to a poor fisherman. The captain would later report that "luggage came on shore from boats untouched, and in all the painful services of that morning these men followed my directions with activity and fidelity."

Somewhat remarkably, the 'first intelligence' of the disaster was brought to the Stock Exchange in Glasgow at two o'clock on the very same day by one of the survivors. The Glasgow Herald said it arrived in the city "like a thunderbolt." Mr Fleming of Stirling Square in the city made an announcement and moments later letters to the Messrs Burns from Captain Henderson and from Captain Dalzell, the agent for the Glasgow underwriters who was at Stranraer, were placed on the bar of the Exchange by the first mate George Langlands. The steamship Fenella had been passing Portpatrick at half past five that morning, just three hours after the wrecking, on its regular route from Fleetwood to Troon. Captain Wheeler was shocked to see the masts and funnel of a wrecked ship and went to the port to see if he could render assistance. Captains Henderson and Dalzell took a small boat out to the steamer and wrote respective letters to the ship owners and to Lloyds, the underwriters. Nineteen survivors who felt able, also joined the Fenella to travel on board to Troon and then to Glasgow by a train hurriedly organised for the purpose. The commander of the Fenella, Captain J J Wheeler, reported to his ship's owners that he had, of course, not charged any of the survivors for the passage, and was able to confirm that to his knowledge all the crew of the Orion were safe apart from the stewardess, the carpenter and an apprentice boy. Like many of his passengers and crew he had clearly been very unnerved by the sight of the wreck. In his report he added: "I am so nervous I can scarcely write so you must make every excuse for my scrawl." No one aboard could understand how the occurrence had happened given the 'beautifully clear' night and the sea 'as calm as a mill pond.' The belief on the Fenella was that the officer on watch must have "endeavoured to pass between the well-known rocks and the shore."

## The letter sent by Captain Henderson to his employers said:

"To Messrs J and G Burns, Gentlemen, It has become my painful duty to announce to you that the Orion struck the rocks a little to the northward of this place this morning at about a quarter past one, and instantly filled, and sunk in seven fathoms of water. From the moment she first struck, the engines became hopeless, and I found it impossible to run her to shore to save the lives of the passengers. I very much fear the loss of life is great, but at present I cannot ascertain the particulars. I have forwarded those passengers who are in a fit state to be removed, to Troon, to Glasgow. I am exceedingly sorry to state that Dr. Burns is among the drowned. His body is now in safe keeping till I know your wishes. I will send this to you by Mr. Langlands, my chief officer, to whom I beg to refer you for particulars. I am, gentlemen, your obedient servant. "

## The letter from the Lloyds Agent, Captain James Dazlell:

Tuesday, Six am.

Dear Sir, being at Stranraer, I was called up during the night to be informed of the loss of the Orion, within a little distance off Portpatrick. I immediately proceeded along with Mr. Irving to her. The loss of life is very great, but in the confusion the number is not yet known. Several of the bodies are now a-landing. The vessel will be a total loss. Her funnel is now only half out of the water. Hull out of sight altogether. Several names have heard of Glasgow persons saved and lost, but I refrain from giving names as the captain of the Orion is writing to the Messrs. Burns. The Fenella called off here to take some of the passengers, and to render assistance."

The more able survivors were keen to continue their journeys, some had joined the Fenella and others like Hugh and George Miller quickly joined the stagecoach from Newton Stewart that was carrying the mail. Nephews of the Provost of Ayr, the two young men were keen to get home before news of the Orion could reach the town and cause unnecessary distress to their family. They were in such a hurry that one of them travelled "without hat, coat, shoes or stockings." With them in the coach was an Irish gentleman who was going to Glasgow by Dumfries and a young Londoner who was so "excited by his escape and sufferings that he persuaded the coachman to stop at Glenluce." The Miller brothers also told a reporter with the Ayr Advertiser that about three miles out of Portpatrick the coach came across a short fair man wearing an Orion uniform and badge running towards Stranraer. He was picked up by the coach and told them he was the man who had been on watch but had been "smoking behind the funnel" when the ship struck. He claimed he was the last person on the wreck having saved the captain and had been sent to Stranraer to find a steamer to take passengers to Greenock, and he duly got out in the town. The Millers were reported to be somewhat sceptical about this story as although he was wearing the uniform, they could not reconcile how he could be the last to leave the wreck and yet be three miles ahead of the mail. To add to this story there were some reports by passengers that members of the crew had later been celebrating their survival in one of Portpatrick's inns, which was generally regarded as in very poor taste given the loss of life.

In homes throughout the village the more seriously affected survivors were being shown the most extraordinary kindness by people who had very little. The whole community had rallied round even though the disaster must have been a terrible experience for them all. Many of the dead were women and young children. One witness said that 'among the most affecting in the house of death were three beautiful children whom no one has identified and whose father and mother must have perished.' Elizabeth Colquhoun and her cousin Mary Houston had tragically lost hold of little James and Mary as they fell into the water. The next time they saw the children they were laid together in the makeshift mortuary.

Generosity was offered by people of every background. Mr and Mrs Hunter Blair of nearby Dunskey House arrived at the village with large supplies of clothes and invitations for survivors to be taken to their country home. It was reported that "by the kindness of this gentleman, at least fifteen persons have been clothed who were almost entirely destitute." Another Lloyds agent, a Mr McClure, gave away every article of clothing in his possession other than the suit he was wearing at the time.

Reverend Clarke found himself in a cottage with a fire blazing in the hearth and he was helped to peel off his soaking clothes. Served with hot brandy and then tea he soon began to warm up, though his teeth continued to "chatter noisily for more than an hour." There were other survivors in the room with him, one also lying in bed and the others huddled round the fire wrapped in blankets, dressed only in their shirts. One was an amputee who had lost his crutch in the panic and was having to hop, somewhat comically, around the room. All were from steerage and were excitedly exchanging stories about how they had escaped death. Two had hung on to ropes until they were picked up by the shore boats whilst the third had managed to swim ashore. The man also lying in the bed was struggling with grief believing that both his master and his son had died in the wrecking. "I little thought that my long service would end this way," he told the clergyman, "he [his master] had gone to bed and was asleep when the vessel struck. When I went and told him what had happened, he immediately got out of bed and put on his drawers and wanted to dress himself. But I said there is no time to dress sir. We must go up instantly and first putting his gold watch inside the waistband of his drawers and taking his gold headed stick with me in my hand, I helped him up the cabin stairs, as well as I could. It was heart rending. All the while he was praying and commending his soul to God. I was with him keeping him up and helping to hold on to the very last. And when I found we were both going I put a rope in his hand and told him to try his best not to let go. Then came the terrible swallowing up of everything and I saw him no more."

After making a few enquiries Reverend Clarke realised that the poor man's master was the gentleman he had seen the previous afternoon and it was revealed that this was Dr Burns, the 76-year-old eminent physician and brother of the Orion's owners. The man's son was one of the crew who had been at the helm two hours before the crash. The reverend's three talkative steerage companions on hearing about the Fenella decided to join those who were going aboard and were quickly furnished with some of their own clothes, which were by then a little drier, or oddments supplied by villagers. It was not long after they had left that Dr Burn's valet was happily reunited with his son – "a young man of about five and twenty in full proper sailor costume and without any signs of having undergone much hardship," Mr Clarke observed.

Whilst moved by this meeting of father and son, the clergyman remained quietly unimpressed with the behaviour of the crew. "That the son should appear so well, and so much as usual in his dress, (ie as if nothing had happened) created no longer astonishment in my mind on hearing that he was one of those who escaped so bravely to shore in the first boat." The sailor claimed that the reason for the wreck was the unreliability of the compasses, a theory that didn't wash with Mr Clarke who privately felt that it was a mistake then to rely on them at all if they were thought to be incorrect. Whether or not this was all a factor in his state of mind, he quickly made enquiries about the possibility of being taken to the home of a fellow clergyman and shortly after this was arranged and he was able to set off, wearing an extraordinary outfit of borrowed clothing including a sailor's cap, towards the home of Portpatrick's Free Church minister, Mr Andrew Urquhart.

Outside in the streets local people were busy dealing with the reality of the disaster that had occurred on their doorstep. The quayside was filled with distressed survivors and relatives, dressed in donated clothes, and anxiously waiting for news of their loved ones. Carts were arriving from the pier laden with drenched boxes, bags, portmanteaux, that were being salvaged as they rose to the surface or were found floating on the water. From a position at the north of the village Reverend Clarke was astonished and bewildered to view the scene of the wreck: "It seemed to me absolutely incredible that any person in his senses could have steered the vessel in such a course – so near and so direct for the shore – to say nothing of the sunken rock on which she had struck. And yet there she was lying, apparently, not 400 or 500 yards from the rocks (I do not know how high) as if she had made right for them."

Mr Clarke was one of several people given support and shelter by the Reverend Urquhart and his family, including the wife and daughter of Mr Roby. They had been taken to the manse to await news and they shared their story with the household. Both women had been amongst the first to dress and hurry onto the deck. When she couldn't see her husband, Mrs Roby had gone to the cabin to alert him, at this time male and female cabins were in separate parts of the ship. When he didn't reply to her call, she assumed he was somewhere on deck but in the desperate confusion she still couldn't see him. Keeping her daughter by her side, Mrs Roby had managed to hang on to a rope at the stern of the ship until they were picked up by the Portpatrick boatmen. She had been confident that her husband would also survive. "He was so strong in the wrists," she stated, "and on other occasions had proved himself of great bodily power that he could not but be among the saved."

Several hours later Rev Urquhart visited what Mr Clarke referred to as the 'house of death' and returned with a ring known to belong to Mr Roby, with the terrible news that he had drowned in the disaster. From marks on his hands and head it was believed that he had been holding on to a rope but been dealt a blow that must have led to his death.

A reporter, who had arrived in the village, was taken to the mortuary by one man whose ten-year-old daughter had been saved, but who pointed to the body of his brother in law who had been in charge of the girl on the voyage. The journalist wrote: "The bodies rescued present one of the most ghastly and melancholy spectacles ever beheld. The bodies claimed are those of Mrs. Splatt and her two daughters, Ann and Mary Ann; Mr. Marchbank, traveller to Messrs. Clapperton and Co., Glasgow; Mr. Bennet, Chester ; Mr. Jago, Liverpool; Mr. Roby; two children of the name of Fraser, from New Brighton, Liverpool—one of these was an infant about 12 months, and the other a child of about three years; Mr. Ross, Glasgow; Alexander Graham, the steward; John Pearce, Liverpool; Mrs. McNeill and two daughters; Harriet McKenzie Peughe a daughter of the Rev. Mr. Peughe of the Episcopalian chapel, Paisley; and Dr. Burns."

At Harbour House, the home of Captain Edward Hawes, more survivors were being comforted and clothed including one young girl who had been travelling home from school with an uncle and other relations, but who had lost all her accompanying family. In his study the commander sat down at his desk to write a letter that would that make the late editions of that day's newspapers.

"Sir, it is my painful duty to report the melancholy loss of life which occurred this morning on the wreck of the Orion steam ship near this place on her voyage from Liverpool to Glasgow and having on board upwards of 200 persons, including crew. The Orion passed close by the lighthouse pier at 1.40am, the weather calm and hazy, and having run with great force on the rocky projection of the coast about 400 yards north of the harbour, rebounded off and sunk in five fathoms of water. So fearfully rapid was this calamity that scarcely seven minutes appear to elapse from the vessel striking until her hull sunk under water, and it is feared that many of the unfortunate sufferers had not time to leave their berths. The circumstances were partly witnessed from the shore, and the alarm being speedily given, the harbour boatmen with every available boat in the port was, with myself, soon at the wreck and it was our unspeakable happiness to assist in rescuing those persons who still clung to the rigging and upper rails of the hull. From information up to this time I have reason to believe one hundred and fifty persons have been saved leaving the fearful number of fifty whose fate is doubtful. I beg to enclose those the names of those survivors who have actually been seen which with 35 of the crew amounts to 140. I feel bound to express my admiration of the activity shown by the boatmen on the part in their exertions to save life and the manner of the inhabitants who gave up their beds and clothing for the sufferers as they landed."

# The initial lists published were:

## Saved

Captain Henderson, George Landlands and his wife Mrs Langlands, Mrs Spense of Liverpool John M A Jones, Mr Edward Alfred Marshall, Wallingford, Berks , Major John Mann East India Ship Company, Richard Price, Master D Darroch son of Major Darroch of Gourock, Thomas Kidston of Mssrs R T Miller and Co of Glasgow, Mr Mrs Miss Anderson, Liverpool, Samuel H Napier and Mrs Napier, Liverpool, W J Walker, Peter McLellan, Copper Street, Liverpool, Mr Valegia, John Roberts, Castle Brewery, Liverpool, Lawrence Barmer, (Banner) Montreal, Mrs Thomson and child of Prescott, Mrs Sucker, Mrs Sucker, Miss S J Sucker, Inverness, from America. Mrs, Miss Roby, Malvern, William Anderson, accountant, John Street, Glasgow, Mr Williams, Liverpool, Mrs Peace, Liverpool, John Archibald, and Master William Archibald, Kellar's Brae, Alloa, George Lamb, Alloa, John Brennan, John Docherty, Liverpool, Mr Mrs Hurst, Liverpool, Mr Mrs Miss Hannah Whitehead of Saddleworth with their daughters Mary and Hannah, Miss Janet Colquhoun Jamieson, Glasgow, Isabella Duncan, Liverpool, James Gibbons, Glasgow, Thomas Devlin, Glasgow, John T Rennie, Aberdeen, Miss Omer, Aberdeen, John McCall, Glasgow, James and Alexander Lyall, 23 St Vincent Street, Glasgow, William Mackenzie Junior, Glasgow, William M Moss, Glasgow, Richard Spenser, Glasgow, Mrs John Pearce, Captain and Mrs McKechnie, Glen, Greenock, Miss Farquharson, Paisley, Joseph Connor, New York, Lawrence, Mrs Gladstone and family, Liverpool, Mr Thomas Williams, Liverpool, Mr John C and Alexander McNeill, Colonsay, Miss White, Carolina Sorely, William Bond, Glasgow, Carolina Martin, Mrs Hunter, Port Glasgow, Elizabeth Colquhoun, Joseph A Pritchard, 7 St George Street, Liverpool, Patrick Marra, Staffordshire, John Biggar, William and Mrs Gardner, 27 Turner's Court, Glasgow, James Walker, Glasgow, John Oldham, Shepton Mallet, Somersetshire, Miss E Woolfield, 28 Buchanan Street, Glasgow, John and Magnus Tait, Baker, John Street, Glasgow, John Walker, John Mills, Liverpool, Henry Thomson, Liverpool, Adam Forbes, Stirling, Robert Bell, Truro, William Kelly, Dartmouth, James Payne, Dartmouth, John Merrilees, Paisley, Duncan Campbell, Glasgow, Peter Ramsay, Liverpool, Mr Mrs Merrilees, Liverpool, Mr Mrs Mary Thomson, 30 Monteith Row, Glasgow, Margaret O'Brien, Mary E Nicholl, Liverpool, John Stewart, 65 Nelson Street, Glasgow, Archibald Oughterson, Dalkeith House, Argyllshire , Caroline Marsden, Saddleworth, Edward and Mrs Hurst, Hamar Hall, Rochdale, Miss E Hurst, Saddleworth, William Drew, Liverpool, William Crichton, Perth, Liverpool, Mr Patterson, Greenock, Mr Fleming and two nephews, Stirling Square, Glasgow, Mr Kelso, Liverpool, Hugh and George

Miller, Ayr, Mrs Langlands, Mr J Campbell, Abercromby, Crieff, Mr John Cameron, of Messrs Clapperton and Co, 175 Trongate, Glasgow, Mr Drysdale, C Jujnot, US, J Lequiez, France, John Robert Campbell, England, Mr Grandison from Mexico, Mr P McIntosh of Messrs Gardner and McIntosh, James Beattie, Edinburgh, James Wade, Edinburgh, Peter Townshend, Accountant, Liverpool, Miss Hessy Jenkins, James Pullar, Dundee, Mr Lyle and son, Glasgow, Mr Mrs Henderson and daughter, Dr and Mrs Nichol and son and daughter, Mr William Paton, Mr Splatt, Hugh McGill, Liverpool, Mr Goldie, Mr and Mrs Robert Buchanan, Glasgow, Mr Thomson, Preston, Mr Philip Alston, Glasgow, Major Freeman, East India Ship Company, Mrs Pears, Lieutenant Maurice Jones, Royal Navy, John James , Master Darrock of Gourock and his tutor, Thomas Kidston, Glasgow, Mr Henry, Mrs and Miss Anderson, Cliftonpark, Birkenhead., Mr W J Walker, Henry Thomson, Liverpool, Andrew [Adam] Forbes, Stirling, Margaret O'Brien, John Docherty, Liverpool, Mrs and Miss Hannah Whitehead, Janet Colquhoun Jamieson, Glasgow, Isabella Duncan, Liverpool, James Gibbons, Glasgow, Thomas Delvin, Glasgow, John T Rennie, ship owner, Aberdeen, Miss Omer, Aberdeen, John McCall, Glasgow, James and Alexander Lyall, Glasgow, William Mackenzie Junior, Liverpool, William M Moss, merchant, Liverpool, Richard Spencer, Liverpool, Peter McLellan, Liverpool, John Roberts, traveller, Dugald Cameron, Glasgow, Miss S Sutter, America, Mr Mrs and Miss J Sucker, Perth, William Priest, Liverpool, James Holt, Royal Navy, Mrs Williams, Liverpool, George and Henry and Mary Lamb, Liverpool, Rev J Clarke, Stretford near Manchester, James Walker, Glasgow, John Walker, Mrs J Pierce, James Connal, New York, Caroline Sorley, Elijah Pinkness, Liverpool, Walter Ewing, Liverpool, Philip McUlstall, Glasgow, Patrick Manna, Staffordshire, Mr Mrs Deuchar and child, Mr W Parsons, Mr Glenlion, Penzance, Mr Dugdale, Miss Louisa Livesley, Liverpool, Master Hutchinson, Mr Cusak, Liverpool.

**Drowned – this is the list later read at the start of the trial of the Orion's officers.**

Alexander McNeill, Ann Carstairs McNeill, Cecil Ann McNeill, Hester Mary McNeill

John Burns MD,

Eliza Morris – niece of Dr Burns

Elizabeth Laskey or Splatt – wife of John Splatt, Devon, Mary Ann Splatt, Anna Splatt

John Roby, Great Malvern, Wiltshire

William Marchbank, Garnet Hill, Glasgow

James and Mary Houston – children of James Houston, shipmaster, Port Glasgow

Harriet McKenzie Pugh – daughter of Rev Kenneth McKenzie Pugh, Paisley

John Hume – wool merchant

James Dunn, apprentice, Orion

Andrew Walker, carpenter

Alexander Graham, steward

Robert Haslam

Mary Ann Adamson or Fraser of New York and her son

David William Fraser.

Thomas Jago, merchant, Liverpool

John Pearce, merchant and ship owner, Mevagissey

Thomas Bancroft Bennet, Chester

Francis McMurrich, coppersmith, Liverpool

Willian Latham, manufacturer of Gillstocks, Little Bolton

James Martin, son of Thomas Martin, Burns and Co, Liverpool

Jessie Underwood or Cassin, wife of John Cassin, blacksmith, Walton near Liverpool

Robert Cassin, son of John and Jessie Cassin

James Scott, merchant, Montreal

Agnes Gladstone, daughter of Lawrence Gladstone, Clifton Park, Birkenhead

The court list ended there adding that there were other names unknown. But the drowned were later known to include

Mr Marchbanks, Glasgow

Miss Nichol, daughter of Dr Nichol, Rodney Street.

A son of Lawrence Gladstone, Liverpool

Elizabeth Gibson, Edinburgh

Owen Pritchard, Liverpool

Two further daughters of John Splatt.

# Chapter Five

*"The bell was not rung, nor the shore hailed."*

Despite the shock and suddenness of the disaster there was an impressive speed to the way the authorities and the press responded. Not only were survivors in Glasgow by the same afternoon, along with letters giving versions of what had happened, but the legal system was also very quick to act. The fiscal, Mr McNeel Caird and two justices of the peace Mr McNeil and Mr Taylor from Stranraer, along with Sheriff McDuff Rhind were all very quickly on the scene. Whilst survivors and villagers wondered how the accident could have happened in such conditions, it was clear there were serious questions to be asked and almost immediately Captain Henderson and his second mate found themselves under investigation. Not only was this a terrible disaster, with several high-profile passengers amongst the drowned, but it was also a very personal loss for the company that owned the vessel. The dead included the ship owners' highly respected brother Dr Burns and niece Miss Morris, James Martin, the 14 year old son of the company's Liverpool agent, and many wealthy well-known merchants travelling for business, along with Captain McNeill, a veteran of the Peninsula War and laird of Colonsay and his wife and two daughters, and a young son of Laurence Gladstone a nephew of politician and future British Prime Minister, William Ewart Gladstone.

Whilst the Orion had been well insured in the Underwriters' Room in Glasgow for £14,500 and the Burns brothers had further policies 'out of the room' to an equal amount, the mitigation of any financial loss could not compensate for the horror of the deaths and the damage to the company's reputation.

One "remarkable circumstance" quickly commented on by the Shipping and Mercantile Gazette, was the fact that no alarm had been sounded by the officers or crew of the Orion when she struck or subsequently "the bell was not rung, nor the shore hailed. There were people who saw the vessel pass the lighthouse and had an alarm been given boats from the shore could have been alongside the vessel some time before her own boats were cleared away and in the water." Of course, the witnesses in the village had acted quickly but the point was valid, that no alarm had been given, the bell had not been rung either to alert those on shore or the ship's own passengers.

The same reporter managed to speak to John Williams, the second mate and he asked him about the disaster: "he informed me Portpatrick was visible enough, and no mist, except a dark cloud, he said, which stood over the flagstaff standing on a rock called McCook's Craig, situated on the northern entrance of the harbour. I inquired his reason for sailing close to shore. His answer was, to keep out of the current; when he saw the rock ahead, he ran to waken the captain, when she struck." While the investigations had only just been initiated many passengers were quite frank about where they felt the fault lay. Survivor Henry Anderson of Cliftonpark, Birkenhead who had been travelling with his wife and daughter told the Liverpool Times: "I attribute the loss of the vessel to mismanagement on the part of the persons in charge at the time, and to an attempt to shave the land finely, with a view of making a quick passage. To the best of my knowledge I never saw a sailor during the whole time of the catastrophe." The family had been saved by jumping 20 feet down from the taffrail into the largest lifeboat. They suffered some bruising and Mr Anderson had joined the other passengers in bailing out the boat with their hats.

The frequency of steamships using the North Channel, the narrow part of the Irish Sea between Scotland and the northern part of Ireland, meant that instructions were being given and received with great speed. The bodies of the dead who had been identified were quickly transported – this was high summer after all. The Princess Royal, another Liverpool to Glasgow steamer arrived at the small port at 3 am the following morning to collect the living and the dead from the Orion. As the survivors emerged from the homes of villagers who had given them support, there were distressing scenes. One man had arrived with the ship from Liverpool to find news of his daughter, believing her to be amongst the lost only to see the girl being helped along the quay by the woman she had been lodged with. One young man whose sister was missing presumed lost, was in a terrible dilemma as he also felt obliged to journey on to reassure their friends of his survival, but at the same time was reluctant to leave before the body was found. Unsure of what to do he was seen repeatedly walking from the steamer to the quay "wringing his hands and crying in bitter agony." Eventually others intervened and encouraged him to leave.

The Princess Royal also carried the bodies of Mr Jago, Mr Pierce, both merchants of Liverpool, and retired banker, Mr John Roby back to the city and the following day, the Commodore from Glasgow called at Portpatrick to collect the body of a Mr Bennett of Chester. Amongst the survivors on board the Princess Royal were the Reverend Joseph Clarke, Mr Mrs Samuel H Napier of Liverpool, Major Mann, Mr Drysdale, Mr Bernie, Mr Glenlion of Penzance, John Robert Campbell, Dr Nicol and his wife, a son and daughter, another daughter had drowned.

At 7 am the Tartar steam-packet, owned by Messrs Burns and carrying James Burns along with the company's marine superintendent Captain Walter

Douglas, an engineer and other officers, arrived in the port with the purpose of making every effort to save the vessel and recover the lost. One reporter noted: "Mr. Bums, the proprietor, had the melancholy duty to perform of looking after the remains of his distinguished brother. Professor Bums, of the College of Glasgow, one of the deceased passengers. The Tartar steamship brought between 20 and 30 coffins. In walking up and down the quay the melancholy spectacle of coffins carried by the seamen to the steam-boats, containing the bodies of the drowned persons, presented itself every now and then." Later in the day, the Tartar returned to Glasgow with several of the coffins now carrying the remains of the drowned including Dr Burns, Mr Scott of Montreal, the young daughter of Reverend Peughe, and the Orion's steward Mr Graham. It steamed along the Clyde with its colours at half-mast and was greeted at Greenock by a huge crowd of people all clamouring to hear news.

Amongst the survivors on the Princess Royal were two men who arrived in Glasgow in a "state of great destitution." They went to the police office for assistance but after being interviewed were sent on to hospital where they were given refreshments. According to the North British Daily Mail one was an elderly man many years senior to his companion, and both had been travelling as steerage passengers. They had seen the proximity of the shore and had assumed the Orion was going to stop at Portpatrick so had gone below to try and find a seat in the packed steerage saloon. They had only been there a few minutes when they heard the crash and the rush of water had thrown the old man to the roof, causing him a concussion. Thankfully, the crush of panicking passengers had carried him through the hatchway. Both men told the newspaper that "the crew were completely paralysed and incapable of action." They saw the captain go up into the rigging and decided to follow – which saved their lives, though they had to cling on for an hour and a half before being rescued.

The Ayr Advertiser wrote that on Wednesday the "town of Stranraer was almost entirely deserted, many of the inhabitants in their anxiety having left for the scene of the disaster, and the streets presented quite a Sabbatical appearance." The ominous quiet was only broken by the arrival of survivors "in a most pitiable predicament, being scantily supplied with clothing, and in the agitation of the moment seeming to have but little idea of where they were."

For some people opening their morning newspapers there must have been the most intense sense of relief that they did not feature in the lists of names. It was reported that the family of one respectable Glasgow banker had been ready to join the Orion but at the last minute their plans had been changed as one of the sons, described as "something of a mechanical genius", had insisted on staying to see some inventions that had come to his attention in the city. "Forced almost against their inclinations to accede to the desires of the young man, the family remained in Liverpool and in this way were preserved from the accident by which so many had perished."

At noon on Wednesday the steam tug, the Defiance, arrived carrying divers from Liverpool who immediately set to work trying to recover bodies and valuables from the wreck. The ship had been carrying wealthy people, "from the highest ranks of society" as one newspaper put it, many at the beginning or final stages of long journeys, who had been carrying, in some cases, a lifetime of savings in gold. The company was keen to salvage something of its reputation from the desperate situation and the police, under the command of Superintendent William Ross, were immediately set to guarding the building where the rescued luggage, and the deceased, were being kept whilst other officers along with members of the coastguard and the Orion's crew were set to protect the wreck site during the night with an armed guard. Police constable William F Thomson was put in charge of looking after the recovered bodies, seeing that their clothing was searched and making every effort to have them identified. If not, he had to ensure their interment in the church yard.

The divers had been tasked with trying to find the missing, and most urgently locate the steward's pantry and the way-bill detailing the numbers of passengers on board that it was hoped would be there, as the steward himself had died. Until a list of was found of how many people had been on the Orion when she set sail, there was no way of knowing how many were still lost.

The *Glasgow Herald* had been extremely critical of the lack of any solid information on numbers. "Until the third day of the accident no list of any authenticity had been made available, while in the small village of Portpatrick this catalogue might have been made by any neutral gentleman present within three hours of the accident. Neither did the steamboat's captain think to furnish lists of the rescued which they themselves brought away. The suspense and anxiety to know the worst or best regarding their relations is almost unbearable."

There is no doubt that the growing criticism of the wrecking and the immediate aftermath added to the pressure felt by those at the scene. For the divers going down to the sunken wreck this was not only a dangerous job but a desperately grim one. The speed with which the steamer had gone down meant that it was highly likely there would be many who had drowned in their sleep or had been trapped by the force and rapidity of the water rushing into the lower decks.

*From the London Illustrated News*

Divers in the mid-19th century wore dry clothes, heavy stockings, guernseys and a woollen hat under a watertight suit, with weighted boots and a heavy copper helmet attached to the ship on the surface by tubes which supplied the diver with air by means of bellows. It was an exhausting and dangerous profession even when employed on routine maintenance but for those at work on the Orion, it was also extremely harrowing. It was going to be a lengthy process – the divers could only go down to the wreck for about three hours a day, at particular times of the tide. The process was well described by one reporter:

"The operation is tedious in itself and, even under the best circumstances, the diver has only three or four hours to work upon each day. The diver wears a large helmet, with its appendages strapped closely over the man's head and body. The helmet is furnished, opposite the eyes, with two large goggles or sight glasses; on the crown or top is a flexible pipe or hose, connected with the boat floating above and which the fresh air is pumped and the foul air out—thus affording ample material for the healthy play of the man's lungs. He is then provided with heavy weights to his shoulders and feet to overcome the buoyancy of the body and keep him steady, and thus accoutred he is ready for work, and let down. Although the diver's operations are necessarily slow, he can penetrate to the most remote nooks, and inspect minute objects. After being down for some time, the man is brought up perspiring most copiously within the enclosure round his head and neck, but chilled and sometimes numbed in his hands and fingers, which are, course, naked and exposed."

Bravely, Superintendent Ross felt that as part of his inquiries he should see the wreck site for himself. With no previous diving experience, he put on the complex and heavy apparatus over several days and went down to investigate what had happened to the Orion. After three hours he discovered the spot where the ship had struck – a considerable distance from the position where it was believed she had been wrecked. He found "large masses of the [Ward] Rock were broken away by the concussion and several sheets of iron which remained there which told the whole truth. It is evident that instead of steaming along the land, the vessel was steered right in for it and when she struck the rocky cliffs must have been broad upon both bows." (1)

There were also plans to try and raise the ship and the vessels the Salamander, Trident and Lucifer were sent by the Lords of the Admiralty led by the highly experienced Captain Caffin with the intention of making an attempt. The captain had something of a reputation after successfully raising a war steamer called The Sphinx after she went down off the Isle of White.

On their first visit to the wreck on the Wednesday afternoon, the divers had managed to go into the fore cabin finding 40 packages of luggage and upwards of £100 in gold. Conditions sometimes made the salvage efforts even more challenging. A ground swell rolled into the coast, so heavy that the diver had great difficulty keeping his feet, though he managed to send up one of the sideboards containing plated ware, silver forks and spoons.

At the foot of the companion stair he discovered the body of a woman identified as Mrs Smith, carrying a gold watch and purse containing 24 sovereigns. She had clearly been overcome by the rushing water in her desperate attempt to reach the deck. This recently widowed woman had been travelling to Glasgow from Montreal with her brother-in-law Mr Scott and his wife and daughter. She had left behind her nine children to visit relatives in the Scottish city, believing she would be returning to them in just a few months' time. The diver also located a further sideboard filled with valuables.

Captain Douglas, the company's marine superintendent, tried to persuade the diver to go down for a second time that day but he refused saying it was too dangerous. In his daily letters to the company he wrote: "I hope they will get it tomorrow if the water is smooth." But in his next report he instead had to explain that the "divers rebelled this morning and would not go out to the wreck though it was arranged and understood by them that the steamer would have steam up ready to go out at two o'clock. Every means was used to induce them to take advantage of the tide as there was not much swell but without effect. This was very distressing to all but particularly those who are assembled here waiting in the hope of recovering the remains of their departed relatives and friends."

Under a great deal of pressure not only from his employers but also from the families, survivors and Press, Captain Douglas appears to have had little sympathy with the difficulties of the divers as he immediately instructed the owner of the apparatus, Mr Bell, to dismiss them. He then sent a representative across to Donaghadee, the Irish port 21 miles across the channel, in the ship the Dunoon Castle to fetch a man he knew to be a diver and he returned by 2 o'clock having succeeded in finding replacements who then immediately went out to the wreck. However, the ground swell was so heavy that they were unable to do anything, as the original team had maintained in the morning. The sea was, in fact, so heavy that the ship's funnel was washed away in the flood tide.

Some progress was made. In order to induce local fishermen to go out to look for salvage, Captain Douglas had offered remuneration for anything saved. One crew returned with the body of Mr Francis Murrach from Alloa, identified by a letter found in his clothing, and a writing case belonging to Mr E A Marshall filled with valuable paperwork. Boatmen had also been instructed to search every corner of the coast between the Mull of Galloway and Corsewell point, though as the days passed the discovery of bodies much further distant would illustrate the power of the currents in this area of the coast.

The reason for the rapidity of the Orion's sinking was very quickly established by the divers. There was a large rent 10 feet long by 2 and a half feet wide just under the starboard sponson (a structure running horizontally along through the paddle box and projecting from the side of the ship). The hole had seriously damaged several compartments of the vessel. This confirmed early speculation reported in the Manchester Examiner from experts who had postured that the damage must have been midship where the largest compartment was housed. The ones to the fore and aft were much smaller and theory had been that the bilge took the rock at the main watertight compartment, smashing the engines and rendering the smaller compartments unable to keep the vessel afloat.

Each day brought news of the divers' distressing work. The steward's pantry was soon found but to everyone's disappointment a careful search had not led to the discovery of a passenger list. The body of Glasgow wool merchant, Mr Hume was recovered from near the wreck, he was carrying money and a bill for £250 payable to the Western Bank. Captain Douglas reported that his body was "not at all disfigured." The bodies of a woman and child, both thought to be steerage passengers because of the coarseness of their clothing, were also brought up. The child had been found in the saloon which was explained by the stewardess, Mrs Blain, who said that many people from steerage had rushed down to the cabins to find blankets after the collision.

Salvaged items included four carpet bags, one belonging to Dr Burns, a sideboard filled with silver ware and a bale of carpeting. The conditions inside the wreck were very difficult. "The divers report being unable to get into the state rooms in the saloon from tables, sofas being jammed up against the doors. There are no bodies in the ladies and fore cabins though they have not been thoroughly searched yet from the cabins being full of beds and bedding floating about and interfering with the search," Captain Douglas wrote.

Efforts were further hampered when an accident happened to the diving apparatus which prevented the men going down. Keen for the searches to resume as soon as possible, the Captain added: "it is important to keep the divers at work as everything depends on them." He was particularly anxious to find the bodies of Captain McNeill, Mrs Scott and her daughter, Miss Morris, the carpenter, the apprentice boy and Master Martin, the son of the Orion's Liverpool agent. It had been thought that "poor young Martin" would be found in the fore cabin, but the divers have failed to find him and there were growing fears that the missing people had been swept away with the strong and rapid tides.

Newspapers had reported that Captain McNeill's brother had very quickly arrived in the port though it wasn't mentioned which one. The Captain's brothers included Duncan McNeill who was a distinguished lawyer, later appointed the Lord Justice-General, and certainly his arrival would have increased the pressure on Captain Douglas to find Captain McNeill's body. The English divers were still being employed, having been shown to be correct in not going down on that occasion by the arrival of the Irish team who then could not dive in the conditions either.

One of the English though had been quite traumatised by one incident described by Captain Douglas: "He has manifested so much reluctance that he could not go down, his feelings having been excited by the presence of the body of an infant as to cause him to give the signal to be hauled up and he has not been down since." Once again Captain Douglas showed himself to be not the most understanding of men by adding that he felt the Irish were much braver.

All aspects of the business of dealing with the aftermath of the tragedy were proceeding with some urgency. Captain Henry Mangles Denham RN, the Inspector General of the Board of Trade had been sent by the British Government to Portpatrick for the purpose of surveying the coast and carrying out his own investigation into the cause of the wrecking. In a letter to the Harbour Department of the Admiralty he later reported that he believed there had been 212 persons on board including crew and that 41 were drowned, with 37 bodies found. "The vessel appears to have been lost through the negligence of the second mate who was in charge as pilot at the time. Both he and the master are committed on charges of neglect of duty and culpable homicide."

Wigtownshire's Procurator Fiscal had also started taking statements for the precognition process, gathering witness statements, as Captain Henderson and the second mate John Williams had been initially imprisoned at Stranraer before being bailed. None of this came as any surprise as most people, locally and nationally, were of the opinion that someone was clearly responsible for the tragedy.

The Glasgow newspaper the North British Daily Mail commented: " The sound and powerful Orion sinking amidst the smooth and placid waters at the mouth of a harbour and in the light and beauty of a summer morning is a spectacle which has little of the divine and inevitable aspect to comfort or compose our minds. It is difficult to account for such a catastrophe on any hypothesis that does not reflect severely the officers in charge of the ill-fated ship." Some of the Orion's crew, including engineers and stokers, had been allowed to leave the village though most of the seamen had been ordered to remain to help with either the guarding of the wreck site or helping to search the inlets and bays.

As newspaper reporters began to arrive at the village, information started to emerge about the stories of the survivors and the lost. The Miller brothers from Ayr were amongst the first to tell of their escape but some stories were heart-breaking. John Splatt, who was given support at the home of the Rev Urquhart, had lost his wife and four daughters, while the McNeill boys had been orphaned with the loss of their parents and sisters. One young woman who had travelled to Liverpool to wish her much loved brother a safe journey as he set out on his first foreign voyage as a sailor, had been returning home on the Orion. On hearing of the ship's wrecking he had journeyed to Portpatrick to find out if she was safe, "his feeling on hearing of her unhappy end may be imagined."

A week after the wrecking, the divers found two more bodies, one was a steerage passenger who was identified by Peter Latham who had travelled from his home in Bolton Le Moor to find out what had happened to his brother, William. Mr Latham had been travelling with two friends, Jonathon Settle and Robert Haslam – both William and Robert had drowned without leaving their bunks. Like many of the deceased, he was buried at Portpatrick in the old churchyard that lies in the heart of the village. There were others buried there who had not been claimed or identified and it was feared never would be, given the number of tourists and travellers from overseas on board. The newspapers published descriptions of those recovered in the hope that a reader somewhere would recognise them from the details of their clothing.

A stout man from Dundee, black coat, black velvet vest and striped trousers.
A stout man, iron grey trousers and velveteen vest.
An aged man about 70.
A stout man with red whiskers, black and white vest, black trousers.
Two children.
Two young females.
An old man with grey whiskers, light grey hair, 17s 8d in silver, one sovereign.
Very stout gentlemen with a letter to Dr J Williamson, St George's Hospital, London. From steerage, fusee box, hair comb, 13 sovereigns, 10s 9d sandy eyebrows, dark whiskers mixed with grey, brown trousers, light blue stockings.
Two steerage, man and a woman age 25 to 30 with a defective eye.
Man 5ft 10ins, black dress coat, black cloth vest, grey tweed trousers, 1/10s.
Female about 14, red merino gown, grey satin stays, found near the harbour.

The description of one of the victims very quickly brought an identification and the resulting sad news for all that knew him. "Old man, silver spectacles, black vest, coat, trousers bound with grey silk tape round the waistband, brown coat, letter addressed to Mr Robert Donaldson, care of William Dickie, 135 Grafton Street, London. He is said to belong to Dundee. He had on him 16s and 10d and a white handkerchief." It was discovered that he had, indeed, belonged to Dundee and he was the addressee – Robert Donaldson, who was a well-known manufacturer of Blackness Road in the city. He was one of the oldest members of the Reverend George Gilfillan's congregation, a minister of some fame in Scotland. Others sadly were buried without being identified due to the deterioration of their bodies. One was a "stout ruddy faced man about 35 or 40, well-dressed," and another was an "elderly lady dressed in a black satin gown and green silk bonnet."

Several newspapers also reported fears that a clown from Franconi's Cirque National de France was amongst the drowned. The famous circus was holding daily shows at its big top tent, known as Franconi's Castle, on Glasgow Green during June and a letter received by the owners indicated that the performer had left Paris and would arrive just in time to take his passage to Glasgow on the Orion. Although his name had not been on any of the published lists of cabin passengers it was likely he had travelled steerage yet he had failed to appear for the performance on the Thursday night. Believing that he must have been amongst the drowned the circus manager had removed his name from the playbill.

The news of the missing clown was widely reported in periodicals around the UK, as was every nugget of information about the Orion. Due to the article appearing in so many newspapers this part of the story had a happy outcome. By good fortune, the man eventually discovered that he was believed to be dead and revealed that he was alive and well in London. Three weeks had passed before reporters wrote of how he claimed that he had been the victim of a crime and had lost all his money to a pickpocket making it impossible for him to pay for his passage on the Orion.

Another good news story was also reported. A Liverpool man had written to his son to say that he intended travelling on the Orion. Believing his father had drowned, the son went to Portpatrick to see if he could identify him amongst the bodies. Unable to find him among the dead, the authorities had been prepared to disinter someone who had already been buried unclaimed, but having been shown the dead man's boots – which had been kept for such a purpose – and hearing the description of the corpse, the son had decided the deceased could not be his father. Believing that his father's body had not been recovered with a "harrowing heart" the son had joined the ship the Admiral which had stopped at Portpatrick to pick up survivors and coffins, only to make a wonderful discovery. His father had been delayed due to unforeseen circumstances and was, in fact, travelling on board the vessel.

*The Orion at low water from the Illustrated London News.*

# Chapter Six

*"They made a coffin from the plank*
*and she has been decently interred."*

The damaged Orion had settled five fathoms down, approximately 30 feet, as "level and as upright as if she was in dry dock." The funnel had been washed away by a heavy groundswell, but the masts remained visible even at high tide, and the tops of the paddle boxes could be seen at low water. The spectacle of the wreck attracted large numbers of visitors who travelled to the village on outings to gawk at the place where so many had drowned and the rock responsible was quickly dubbed Orion's Rock. Meanwhile, the work of salvaging property, and the search for the lost, continued. All recovered luggage had been forwarded to Stranraer to then be shipped aboard the Briton to be taken to the offices of Messrs Burns in Glasgow.

A letter about the wreck site written by Lieutenant W W Oke of the Royal Navy was made public in the Illustrated London News. The Lieutenant had been the commander of one of the steamships carrying the mail between Portpatrick and Donaghadee and knew the whole coast well between Corsewell and the Mull of Galloway. He wrote: "The Captain of the Orion, I observe, reports her 'to have struck a little to the northward of Portpatrick' and as the charts show deep water there I deem it not out of place to apprise you that, of my own knowledge, there is a ledge of rocks there known and locally called by fishermen the 'Bushes' running out at least 150 yards or more from shore: there is no beacon or buoy on them, but I have myself sounded these rocks." His words hammered home to readers just how close the Orion had been sailing to the coast in order to hit this collection of rocks.

Although some hopes had remained to try and raise the ship using chains the situation had been thought unlikely within days. Captain Douglas had written to the Burns brothers that the idea of lifting her was really a "hopeless case." The captain had visited the site along with Captain Dalzell, the Lloyds agent Mr Irvine, and the foreman of Barclays and found the tops of the paddle boxes awash at low water and he expressed the difficulty of trying to raise such a heavy vessel on such an exposed rocky coastline.

A fortnight after the Orion had gone down the weather changed and there was a heavy gale which swept away all signs of the vessel above the water and below, she began to break up. The masts fell and large pieces of her deck and the woodwork of the cabins floated away. All hopes of raising the vessel were then completely dashed. The action of the storm also brought harrowing results. The body of Captain McNeill was finally discovered floating near the wreck site having been brought up to the surface by the swell. He was found to be carrying £23 in gold, 14s in silver, a gold watch and a knife with A McNeill engraved on it.

Whilst in the village and the whole of the Rhins, people remained focused on the appalling tragedy of the wrecking and the fact that many people had yet to be found, in the rest of the country the story of the Orion was being used for quite blatant advertising and fraud. A band of strolling musicians from England were brought before the Western District Police Court in Glasgow charged with the crime of falsehood, fraud, and wilful imposition after claiming to be survivors of the Orion. The three men, John Brannan, John Evans, and Charles Smith had told a coffee house owner that they had lost everything and, by this, gained their lodgings at a cheap rate. They had also managed to get a gill of whisky from a spirit dealer with the same story.

In another case, Robert Miller from Berwick upon Tweed, claimed he was related to the Provost of Ayr and, like the Provosts' real nephews, had survived the sinking but been left penniless. A spectacle wearing young man claiming to be called Lawrence Banner was charged with attempting to obtain money from the public under false pretences, after saying that he had been a passenger on the Orion and had lost all his property. He had left a printed letter at every house in the area where he was living making this claim and asking for assistance. Unfortunately, one of the houses belonged to a police officer who investigated further. He was found guilty and ordered to serve a month's hard labour. (1) There was also wrongdoing in Portpatrick as a bale of cloth containing four rolls of 50 yards each was taken from the Government yard. The crime surprised locals as one of the Orion's crew had been charged with keeping watch on the yard at night.

Advice to future passengers of paddle steamers was also forthcoming. The Era newspaper ran an article telling people how to create a simple float "in such case of shipwreck as that of the Orion." They were advised to simply take a pocket handkerchief or towel and place a hat in the centre on its crown, gather up the corners and tie together over the centre of the opening – in this way a life buoy is created. By keeping the crown upwards and holding on to the knotted portion it would support a weight of 20 pounds, "much more than sufficient to sustain a person's head and shoulders above the water." This simple instruction came too late, obviously, for the people on the Orion, though even if they had been aware of its possible aid they would have had little time to find hats and handkerchiefs – fifteen minutes after the ship hit the rock it was at the bottom of the sea.

The North British Daily Mail also ran an article saying that Captain Denham's inquiry should also be allowed to suggest improvements to steam vessels that would ensure the safety of passengers. They had a few suggestions of their own "Boats should be hung to be available at once. Buoys and other expedients should be provided, and the management of boats ought to become a special part of training on board steam vessels." The writer pointed out that in the case of the Orion, no guns had been fired to alarm residents and that such signals "ought to be always ready for use." The newspaper argued it was the responsibility of the ship's owners, not only a matter of duty alone, for precautionary arrangements to be adopted.

The Glasgow Herald, within only a few days of the sinking also ran a piece relating to the "public's attention painfully aroused by the shockingly fatal wreck of the Orion" but the article was really an advertisement for a buoyant mattress invented by a Mr R W Laurie. The mattress had been designed for passenger berths, masters, mates and crew, to be used as cushions on benches and sofas. The device was composed of a series of four or more tubes made of waterproofed cloth, inflated with air, divided into compartments, and surrounded by cotton wool and cased in field cotton.

At Portpatrick the storm at the beginning of July had moved not just the body of Captain McNeill but the remains of several more of the missing. Over the next few days bodies began to be washed ashore along the coast and there were some grim discoveries for local people. On one day three were found, a toddler of about 18 months, a man later identified as a Mr Pritchard and the missing child of Dr Nicol who had been waiting at Portpatrick for weeks hoping for news. He immediately arranged for his young daughter to be buried in the churchyard, where the other two bodies were also interred. They had all been in a "frightful state."

The following day a woman's body was discovered floating almost abreast of Dunskey Castle to the south of Portpatrick. She was assumed to be a Miss Adamson as she had that name along with "No 5 1848" written in her clothing, one arm was "marked with Indian Ink" and she was carrying £4. She was also buried in the churchyard.

As the days passed the likelihood of identifying victims diminished and when several more bodies came ashore on the 20th of July, they were terribly disfigured, distressing for those making the macabre discoveries and having to deal with the corpses, and, of course, for the families.

A week or so earlier two bodies, believed to have come from the Orion, had washed ashore as far away as the Isle of Man and had been buried there. The crew of The Tiger reported seeing two bodies floating off the Mull of Galloway but were unable to retrieve them from the sea. A "lad of about 15" was found ashore at Ardwell Bay to the north of Portpatrick dressed in blue trousers, blue vest and a white cotton shirt but his pockets were empty nor name in his clothing to give anyone a clue as to who he was.

For one poor unidentified woman her final resting place was even further away. The Coleraine Chronicle reported that the body of a woman, supposed to have been "one of the sufferers in the ill-fated Orion" was found in the west point of Rathlin Island by some poor fishermen from Ballintoy on the north coast of Ireland. "There was very little covering on the body, but the feet and legs were clothed in black sateen boots very neatly made and fine cotton stockings marked No 10. Near the place was a plank belonging to the cabin of a ship. The men behaved in a most praiseworthy manner as they immediately abandoned their fishing and returning to land, they made a coffin from the plank and she has been decently interred in the church yard of Ballintoy."

One of the drowned discovered during this period was a daughter of John Splatt, identified as Elizabeth from the general description of her dress matching the details given by her father to the police. One daughter was still missing along with family's life savings which had originally been thought to have been sewn into Mrs Splatt's dress but were later said to be in a box. The reporter of the North British Daily Mail wrote at the end of July that there were incorrect reports appearing in some newspapers that Mr Splatt's money had been recovered. "This is quite incorrect," he reported, "and it would be well were you to contradict the statement as it will no doubt be the means of raising the old man's hopes which would be a great pity as the poor old man would feel the loss doubly in being disappointed." The journalist believed he had kept a correct account of the numbers of bodies recovered and by that date had counted 46.

As the plans to raise the vessel had been abandoned, the remains of the hull and its engines were sold by public auction in the village and purchased by a Mr McClure of Portpatrick for £330 – a considerable sum, about £45,000 today. As the time passed the divers were still going to the wreck site daily to salvage some of the valuable and personal items that had been lost, and now also to recover any portable internal fittings for the new owner. Some of the luggage found was incredibly poignant. A silver tea and coffee service had been brought to the surface and found to be inscribed: "Presented to Mr and Mrs Scott on their leaving Canada by a few sincere friends." By terrible coincidence, the body of a woman believed to be Mrs Scott had been found only a few days before at Ballywater near Donaghadee.

Although there were many dead, the tragedies that had befallen several families were particularly heart-rending. The Scotts travelling to visit family in Glasgow after many years in Montreal, the Splatt's journeying with the intention of finally emigrating to join older children for a new life in Australia, and the McNeill's on their way home to Jura and the tiny island of Gigha for the summer. Just a few days after the sinking the *Glasgow Herald* carried a short report of a pleasure trip on a paddle steamer that had sailed near Jura: "Old Sinclair, the pilot pointed out a house beautifully situated facing the water. It was the house of Captain McNeill of Colonsay who with this lady and two daughters, perished on the Orion. As he was on his way home to Jura, the pilot deemed it probable his yacht would have been ordered to wait on him as usual at Crinan, a distance of about ten miles across the sound."

When the family did finally return the article in the Cheltenham Chronicle, though widely reported across the nation's newspapers, was even more moving. "The body of the late Captain and Mrs McNeill and their two daughters were conveyed by the steamer Briton from Stranraer to West Tarbet where the vessel was met by a large number of near relatives and friends and then proceeded to the family burying ground on the island of Gigha. On nearing the island each of the bodies was placed in a separate barge and rowed ashore. At this time the neighbouring land was covered with multitudes of Highlanders who had come to see the last sad rites performed over those who they had revered and loved; the scene was a most painful and affecting one."

# Chapter Seven

*"It was a course full of risk and requiring great skill*
*and yet at this time the captain left the deck."*

At the beginning of August Captain Thomas Henderson, his first mate George Langlands and the second mate John Williams were all indicted for trial at the High Court of Justiciary in Edinburgh at the end of the month, charged with culpable neglect of duty and loss of life. The precognition process had been one of the most extensive in Scottish legal history and the indictment contained reference to more than 80 witnesses, though less than thirty would be called during the trial.

At the same time, a new Mercantile Marine Bill had been making its way through the House of Lords. The bill had three main objects in view, The Globe newspaper reported, firstly that every man who was appointed to the command of ship should prove that he was not deficient in those qualifications that were necessary to the efficient discharge of his duties. Secondly, that any man who had lost a ship through misconduct, or otherwise acted with gross impropriety, should be deprived of his certificate, and should be prevented from commanding a ship in future. And thirdly, "the establishment of recognised shipping offices between the sailor and his employer, by which all the evils attending the existing system of crimping [a means of often hoodwinking crew for ships that were short-handed] be entirely removed." One member of the House expressed his belief that if the Bill had been in operation the Orion would not have been wrecked, and those who had lost their lives would have been saved.

Every day, news of the Orion disaster served to illustrate the need for improvements to the shipping industry, argued the leader writer at the Aberdeen Herald and General Advertiser commenting on the Bill. "The principle of laissez-faire has been too long and too extensively the case in reference to shipping as well as other matters and we are reaping the consequences in frequent accidents arising from carelessness or incompetency of masters and officers and the neglect or cupidity on part of their owners. We trust the powers of inspection conferred by the new and former Acts will be duly enforced and that influenced by a proper appreciation of the loss that has been suffered and the risk that has been incurred from recent accidents which might have been avoided, the parties interested will throw no obstacle in the way."

The British Government also had an inquiry in progress looking at the number and dimensions of lifeboats available for passengers on seagoing steam vessels at different ports in Scotland which commentators believed had been prompted by the loss of the Orion, and following the trial of the ship's officers this would have even greater relevance. Although thousands of passengers travelled daily on steamers around the coast of the UK, either for pleasure or business purposes, the wrecking of the Orion had made travellers understandably nervous.

Only a month after the Orion, another ship owned by the Burns brothers got into difficulties. On the 20th of July, the London Evening Standard stated: "we regret to announce an unfortunate accident on Loch Lomond. About three o'clock to-day the Pilot, one of the steamers carrying excursion passengers up the Loch, while making a trip, suddenly struck on a sunken rock within a short distance of the shore near Ross Point, south of Rowardennan. The shock was so violent that many of the passengers were upset on deck, and the greatest alarm and excitement prevailed. The sensation felt by those on board was as if the vessel was being sawn asunder. The first shock was so sudden that the machinery was not stopped, and no sooner had it been felt than another succeeded. The alarm now felt was greatly increased. The Pilot immediately afterwards reached deep water, and the captain, with great presence of mind, steered the vessel direct for the shore, which he succeeded in reaching without danger, bringing the steamer aground in the bay between Ross Point and Rowardennan. No lives were lost."

But in mid-August Messrs Burns were again in the news when another of their steamers, on a voyage from the west end of the Crinan Canal to Oban, ran into trouble. As it navigated the narrow strait between Easdale and Seil Island, a lady's dress became entangled with the chain mechanism attached to the rudder, causing it to move. "From this trifling cause, which partly tore the gown from her person," reported the Newry Examiner and Louth Advertiser, "the steamer was driven off her course and before the engines could be reversed she struck a sunken rock to the alarm and horror of all on board." The passengers reacted with terror, all being familiar with what had happened to the Orion. Luckily there were several boats to hand and the women and children were all removed from the vessel but the reporter commented that "several gentlemen, some of the most valiant looking men of a large breadth of moustache exhibited symptoms of most painful trepidation and the veteran Lord Gough, the hero of Goojerat, distinguished himself by urging these timid gentlemen to give precedence to the ladies and children." With many of the passengers removed, the vessel then gradually worked its way off the rock and continued on its journey with the women and children returned on board. "Some passengers suffered considerably from the effects of their fright and consternation."

In the Rhins, specialists had arrived from Portsmouth to fully examine the rock struck by the Orion in order to prepare a full report for the trial of the ship's commander and officers. Sadly, bodies were also still being discovered two months after the sinking. The body of a man washed up at Barncorkie Bay near Port Logan and was interred, unidentified, at Portpatrick. It was believed to be the Orion's carpenter but details of his clothing were published in the hope that this could be confirmed by a family member: "dark green and blue tartan trousers with a pair of moleskin trousers beneath, flannel shirt and striped cotton shirt."

There was also a story, widely reported, of one unfortunate man who had been one of the survivors of the Orion's wrecking, only to drown in somewhat bizarre circumstances only a month later. Thomas McNamara, a cart man, had been filling a barrel with water in the river behind the Thomond Gate Distillery in Limerick. The horse drawing the cart backed into the river and the man, horse and all had been carried away and drowned by the river's current.

Although all the preparations had been made for the trial of the officers, there were some eleventh-hour logistical difficulties when it was announced that Queen Victoria would be visiting the Scottish capital during the time the trial was being held. The arrival of the Queen and her entourage in the city prompted concerns for the accommodation of the many witnesses who were travelling from all over the UK at the same time as the city was having to cope with an influx of visitors hoping to catch sight of their monarch. Such was the interest in the Orion that during the Queen's visit her Home Secretary, Sir George Grey, who was one of the accompanying party, went to the High Court to watch some of the much talked of trial.

## The Trial – Day One

Proceedings began on the morning of the 29th August 1850 at the High Court in the heart of Edinburgh's Old Town, with The Lord Justice Clerk, who at that time was Lord Hope, Lords Wood, and Ivory on the bench. The prosecution was led by the Solicitor General, James Moncrieff, assisted by George Deas, who was later to become a notorious hanging judge, and Mr Montgomery Bell supporting. The defence advocates were Mr James Crauford, for the captain, Mr A S Logan for Langlands, and Mr Penney for the second mate. The jury was impanelled and Henderson, Langlands and Williams were all charged with culpable homicide, as also the culpable and reckless neglect of duty by any officer or mariner employed or engaged on board of a ship by which the ship is wrecked, and any of the lieges are bereaved of life. As also the culpable and reckless neglect of duty by any officer or mariner employed or engaged on board of a ship whereby any of the lieges who have embarked on board of said ship are bereaved of life or have their lives exposed to imminent danger.

The very lengthy details of the charges were then read, citing Henderson and Williams in reference to the reckless and dangerous way in which the ship was steered, the failure to have sufficient look-outs stationed at the bows, the captain's reckless neglect of duty in going to retire, but referring to all three men in relation to the poor state of the ship's four lifeboats, their failure to have sufficient oars and bungs. The charges included the names of those known to have drowned, the number stated as 47. After the naming of some of the drowned the reading of the charge concluded with; And you the said Thomas Henderson and John Williams are, both and each, or one or other of you, guilty of the culpable bereavement of the lives of all and each or one or more of the said persons drowned in manner above or libelled and you the said George Langlands, are guilty of the culpable bereavement of the lives of all and each one or more of the said persons drowned in manner above or libelled when left in the sinking ship in consequence of the said boats, or some of them, not having proceeded with passengers from the said ship to the shore as often, before the said ship sank, as they would have done if fully and properly equipped and in consequence, of the said boats for some of them being unfit to carry, or not having carried the full complement of passengers to the shore, or when thrown into the water by capsizing or swamping the quarter boat and life boat capsized or swamped. (1)

All three men, referred to as pannels in that period, pled not guilty with their defences read. Mr Crauford said, the captain claimed that no man could lament more than him the loss of the ship he commanded and the lives of the passengers under his care. He denied the accident was caused by any neglect, reckless or culpable on his part and he could not profess to explain the causes which may have led to the result. He alleged that be had gone below to take a little rest, leaving the vessel in the charge of competent officer, and that after this the accident arose, from circumstances which he could not control. Mr Crauford also said that it was not truly charged against the pannel that he was neglectful of duty in regard to the equipment of the vessel or boats.

Mr Penney for the second mate set forth that he had steered the vessel to the best of his judgment, and that the accident had arisen from the deficient state of the ship's compasses or other machinery, and that he, therefore, was not liable. He also said that the pannel was not responsible for the condition of the boats; but these, he believed were in a perfectly sufficient state. A model of the Orion along with one of the lifeboats were both lodged with the court.

The first witness called for the Crown was Captain Gipp Robinson of the

Royal Navy who had used his extensive maritime expertise to prepare a chart marked with the coastline of the Rhins between Portpatrick and Blackhead and Cromack Point with reference to the tides, channels, and the safe course a steamer should take to avoid hazards. The Outer Ward Rock, where the Orion had hit, lay 1048 feet from the south end of the pier, this rock is always covered by water though the Barnoch Rock, lying 1850 feet away, was visible at low tide. The port paddle had been measured as lying at 475 feet from the Outer Ward Rock, and 500 feet from the Barnoch Rock with a current of tide running directly from this point to the wreck.

The Orion was lying at a depth of 34 feet at the bow and 43 feet at the stern. In a flood tide, the course of the current is southward. In answer to a question from the Lord Justice Clerk the Captain replied: "I do not think that anyone with his eyes open would keep a vessel within its own length of Portpatrick pier. No course compatible with safety could have allowed the vessel to be so near the coast as where she is lying now. The harbour lighthouse is indifferent, but it is seen four miles off in a reasonably fine night." He explained to the court that the current runs to the south at about two knots an hour, increasing towards Cromack Point with the effect that it sweeps a vessel off the point but as it gets nearer to Portpatrick it takes her more inshore, "of course, it is a well-known rule and a person acquainted with the currents must make allowance." Captain Gipp Robinson was also examined in relation to tides, currents and routes taken by vessels sailing this coastline.

The second witness, John Robertson, the manager of Caird & Co, the engineering and shipbuilding company based in Greenock which was responsible for building the Orion, provided details of the ship and described her as being 200 feet in the keel, 210 feet in the fore reach, the depth of hold was 18 feet 6 inches, and 28 feet on the beam. The height of the main mast 44 feet 6 inches with a 400-horsepower engine. He had prepared the model of the Orion, with a cross section to show the five water-tight compartments. The next witness, John McDonald, a Greenock boat builder had prepared the model of one of the lifeboats telling the court that each boat on the Orion should have been able to carry between 70 and 80 passengers.

Seaman David Walker was then called to the witness box where he stated that he had been at the helm between 10 and 12 o'clock under the watch of the first mate along with Charles Niven, George Williams, John Kerr and Adam Walker with Captain Henderson, the first mate and the carpenter also on deck. It was a fine night, a little cloudy with a haze over the land at the Mull of Galloway which they made a little before 12, the light visible through the fog. He thought they were unusually near the coast and had been steering

NNW when, just after midnight, he gave the helm to John Kelly. He told the court that in fog they would use the compass and take the course from the officers. After giving the helm to John Kelly, he went below to rest. When the Orion struck, he had helped with the boats, saying that the problem with launching them had been the stiffness of the tackle and the weight of the passengers, perhaps more the latter.

Under cross examination he said that the bridge above the paddle boxes was higher on the Orion than in most boats and it gave a good view across the bows. He also said that there had been an exercise led by the first mate where the boats had been lowered to check the tackle was working well but earlier in the year the ship had been docked at Le Havre for about a month and covers had been fitted. He added that if the boats had been empty on the night of the wreck there would have been no problem lowering them. Walker also said that as he came up on deck after the collision, he had heard Mr Langlands calling on the crew to launch the lifeboats.

The helmsman, John Kelly, who had been on the Liverpool to Glasgow route for four years, previously under Captain Main, then took the stand and confirmed the weather conditions and gave his opinion of their proximity to the coast. "We were particularly close; I never was so close." He said that he had been given several commands from the second mate to adjust the direction of the Orion, each time taking them a little closer to shore. Kelly had also observed the captain look at the compass and speak with the second mate, who was now in charge of the watch. South of Portpatrick, Kelly was given the command N ½ W, which took the ship out a little, and he overheard an exchange between Wilson and John Williams when the seaman said: "John do you no see land there?" Kelly told the court that they had been alongside Portpatrick sooner than usual. "We had had a good run. Our passage might have been 15 or 16 hours to Greenock, enabling us to run the tide, going to Glasgow with the same tide. We might have been at Greenock about eight o'clock. The tide would turn about an hour after, if we are not there by then we might lose the tide."

He was at the helm when there was the shout of "hard starboard" from a man who sounded clearly afraid, followed by another cry of "land right ahead" from Duncan Campbell standing near the mizzen mast. Kelly told the court that the second mate had run to where the skylight of the captain's cabin was and then back to the helm to help pull the wheel hard to starboard, but moments later the ship hit the rock with a "long, loud crash." He gave detailed evidence about his actions helping to get the larboard boat launched and his efforts to save passengers. Kelly explained that he had never seen lifeboats fastened up the way that the captain had ordered, adding that he believed they had only been lowered twice in the last twenty months. He said that even under normal circumstances and without the hindrance of the cover, with the davits and lockets it would take ten to fifteen minutes to lower the boats. He also said that the variations of the compasses, which had increased after Le Havre, were often a topic of conversation amongst the crew. Kelly told the court that that along with Langlands, he had discovered the body of Dr Burns and taken it to land. Under cross examination from Mr Crauford, Kelly said that he had served under Captains Main and McKellar, and both had stayed on deck longer than Captain Henderson. In answer to a question from Mr Logan he said that lifeboats generally did have covers, though in some vessels they were kept keel up.

Robert Wilson, the Clyde pilot, who had served on the vessel for more than two years, was the next to give evidence. He had been on look-out taking over from James Donald, and he was standing on the gangway, along with James Stewart when the Orion was wrecked. He arrived on deck for the second watch at a quarter past twelve, and land was in sight, the ship less than half a mile from shore and she went closer still. He twice left his position to speak to Williams about the proximity of the coast. "I asked if he saw the land, he said he did but nothing else." He then spoke to Stewart about, what he at one point described as, the "dark loom of the land." He reported Portpatrick light fifteen or twenty minutes before the vessel struck. At 1 am the captain had appeared on deck and told both men on watch to keep a "bright look-out." As the collision became clear Wilson helped with the boats before being saved by one of the funnel stays. He mentioned that as well as the boats there were a number of cork fenders and when the starboard boat capsized, he helped the first mate to lower a large square shaped one into the water. He also agreed with previous evidence about the ship's compasses saying that there was a point difference between the one at the bridge and the one at the binnacle.

Lookout, James Stewart was called next. He described himself as a 'regular' sailor with little experience of being on steamers and had only been with the Orion for a month. His testimony was similar to everything that Wilson had said. He disagreed, though, with earlier opinions about the passengers being the cause of the difficulty with the lifeboats. He had also helped with the starboard boat and felt it had been "jammed" in the chocks, not the fault of those within it. He said that there was a great deal of confusion though he had seen the first mate doing all he could.

Portpatrick fisherman, David Adair, was the first of the villagers to give evidence and spoke of how he had seen the Orion passing unusually close to the pier as he sat in his waterfront home baiting lines. Knowing the coast well he ran to see if the ship had hit the Ward Rock and finding it had, began to raise the alarm. He told the court: "In running down to Ward Bay, I expected to see her strike; and even if she had not struck, she could not have weathered the point of the coast. When I first saw her there was plenty of time at the speed she was then going, to have cleared the coast if her course had been altered." As he dismissed the witness, his Lordship said: "Well, my man, you seem to have acted with great presence of mind, and I have no doubt was instrumental in saving a great many lives."

John Samson Oke, who like David Adair lived near the pier, had been reading when he heard the steamer, and thought she was heading into the harbour she was so close. Deciding to dress to see if there had been accident, he had not even left the window when he heard a "long double crash" and called out 'steamer ashore.' In the five years he had lived in Portpatrick he had not seen a steamer so closer to shore, even when they were landing passengers. A third neighbour, David Armstrong, who gave evidence next, also spoke of the nearness of the vessel, believing that if he had been at the end of the south pier he would have been able to throw a stone that would have hit her. With his daughter he had gone to help raise the alarm.

The Orion's second steward, John McHaffie, confirmed that there had been 115 cabin passengers on board that night but there had been no way of knowing the exact number of steerage travellers, though the average was between 40 and 60, and he guessed there had been nearer 40. He was followed by the Superintendent of Police at Stranraer, William Ross who said that he had arrived on the morning of the wreck and found several dead bodies. After he arranged for the use of an empty property, nineteen bodies were taken there that day though subsequently the number of drowned had since increased to "between 40 and 50 in all." Borrowing a diving "dress" he examined the Ward Rock and found some pieces of iron (which were produced in court) and broken stone. There were a great many fractures and fragments, all on the outside towards the open sea, including one fresh fracture 14 feet in length by 12 to 13 feet in depth. He had also made a model of the fractured rock which was presented to the court. Supt Ross added that there were no fractures on the Barnoch Rock.

William Knott, a seaman and diver from the HM Experimental Gunner ship, the Excellent based at Portsmouth appeared next and agreed with the information given by the police officer. Captain Edward Hawes, the harbour superintendent at Portpatrick then took the stand and spoke of how he had been in charge for some time of the packets that sailed between the port and Donaghadee. He said that in his experience as a naval commander, the plugs in a lifeboat were attached by a lanyard, and the boats themselves were not covered.

The first of several ship commanders then gave evidence about general practice on steamers. They included Dugald Turner of the steamship the Clarence which ran between London and Leith though he had previously worked on the Liverpool to Greenock station, James Murray, a first-class Clyde pilot who had also commanded vessels in the merchant service, James Morrison also a Clyde pilot and former commander, and Abraham Parkes a lieutenant in the Royal Navy who had recently commanded the Dasher, one of the Portpatrick steam packets. Captain Turner said that although there were no general or company rules about a commander remaining on deck, he considered what was important was the safety of the passengers when travelling along the coast. He confirmed that the captain was responsible for the boats and the course of the vessel. During the years he had been on the Liverpool to Greenock route he had never been closer than a mile and a half to this stretch of coastline, even when stopping for passengers at Portpatrick.

James Murray also stated that when running along the coast a captain was bound to keep to the deck whatever the weather. James Morrison explained the two watches, and that if a ship did not have a second officer then a member of the crew was selected for the captain's watch. Lieutenant Parkes said that from Cromack Point, the most projecting headland, taking a course of N ½ W should take a vessel a mile off Portpatrick. "Certainly, it was not proper for the commander of a large steamer running along shore to be found anywhere but on the deck."

"In a strong spring tide, you would gain something by keeping near shore, thereby avoiding the strength of the tides but in a neap tide there was no advantage." He also said that, "if the variation of a compass is known, it ought only to induce the captain to steer by the one most correct." The court then adjourned for the night and began again at nine o'clock the next morning.

**Day Two**
Portpatrick labourer Patrick Horner was the first to take the stand on the Friday morning. He recollected hearing the alarm that a steamer was ashore and went to give help, finding a lifeboat just landing as he arrived at the harbour. The boat was half full of water and had to be bailed out with a hat. As they tried to relaunch it something snagged on the rocks and it was found to be one of the davits still attached. He was followed in the witness box by the keeper of the Mull of Galloway lighthouse, James Scott Brown and his assistant Lawrence Fernier, who both said there had been a fog at the headland from twenty past nine until a quarter to twelve and the steamer had been heard about ten minutes before she passed, about a quarter mile from the coast. The keepers' record book for that night read "south, breeze, fog."

Called to give evidence about the compasses was nautical instrument maker John Gray from Liverpool who had been the supplier to the Orion in July 1847. On March 20th1850 he had adjusted the compasses and again at the end of May he had a conversation with Captain Henderson who told him they were wrong. He told the court that he went on board and made a bet that they were right, and after examining them again, he won the bet. Questioned by Mr Penney, Mr Gray went into some detail to explain the various factors that could affect them, including local attraction from iron, though generally any difference would be due to vibration. He generally found the compasses on the Orion to agree within a degree. He was followed by William Carter, who as a diver had examined the damage done to the Orion by the collision. He had measured a great hole in the starboard bilge, four feet broad and six feet high, with a rent about twenty feet. He had also found bodies in the cabin there.

The final witness for the prosecution was Miss Elizabeth Colquhoun, who was the only survivor from the passengers to be called, despite several being listed. She had been travelling with her cousin and the woman's two young children. Her cousin was unable to attend court as she was still "indisposed." She described the confusion when the ship hit the rock and how they had lost hold of both children when the vessel had fallen over broadside. The next time she had seen the infants was in the mortuary. This essentially concluded the evidence for the prosecution.

The declaration of Captain Henderson made in the presence of Mr A McNeel Caird Esq, the Procurator Fiscal at Stranraer was then read to the court. The accused could not give evidence in their own behalf in 1850. On the evening of the 17th June the weather had been fine with a north west wind. The vessel passed the Mull of Galloway at midnight when the watch changed. There were two look-outs beside the man at the helm and the officer [the second mate] on watch. He saw them all at their posts before he retired to his cabin. At the time the vessel struck he was lying sleeping on his sofa in his own cabin. He did not consider it his duty in the state of the weather and the position of the vessel to be on deck at that time. He was in a state of fatigue and needed rest. He was aroused by the shock and rushed on deck to discover the vessel had struck a rock. He thought that the collision had happened because of a miscalculation by the second officer of the distance between the vessel and the land. After the accident he exerted himself as much as possible to save the lives of the passengers and, as far as a man can do, felt he had done his duty.

He had seen that the starboard lifeboat had been swamped but he was unaware of how many boats had reached shore with passengers; "In the grey of the morning it was difficult to distinguish between the shore boats and their own." He had gone up the rigging and stayed there while the top of the masts remained above water and until he saw all of the passengers clear of the wreck. He was the last to leave. He had left special instructions to be called if there was a change in the weather. When the ship struck, he had stripped so that he could swim ashore and was nearly naked when taken off the wreck.

The declaration of John Williams, also made in the presence of the Procurator Fiscal of Stranraer, was then read to the court. He stated that he was on deck a few minutes after midnight to take his watch and the captain had remained until half past twelve. On leaving he had said: "John, if it becomes any way thick or hazy mind and give me a call." When the vessel was off the pier of Portpatrick it suddenly became thick. He could see the pier quite distinctly at first but when he saw the fog come on he gave orders to John Kelly, who was at the helm, to keep the vessel north by west, a half point off from the land. He was going to call the master when the vessel struck. He could not understand how the accident happened unless the current had swung the vessel inshore against the helm. He kept the vessel near the shore for the purpose of shunning the tide. The master gave him no order to do so on this occasion. He remained on board until the ship went down and was saved from the rigging.

The Solicitor General then stated that he had expected to be able to fix on the first mate, Langlands, an independent responsibility in regard to the state of the boats, and therefore he had been included in the indictment along with the captain and second mate, but the Crown had not found that separate responsibility to exist to the extent expected and the charge against him was withdrawn. The jury returned a verdict of not guilty against Langlands and he left the bar. As a former co-accused he was now available to be called as a witness on behalf of either of the two men who remained in the dock.

Mr Crauford then called a number of ship's captains to give evidence regarding the best course to take along the Scottish coastline, and the practice of taking rest during a voyage. Captain Johnston, harbour master at Glasgow and a sailor for more than forty years, said he had known Thomas Henderson since he was a boy. He said his character was unimpeachable, he was a clever, active sailor and a steady, sober man. Captain John Boyd, a retired commander from the company of Thomson and McConnell explained that it was usual to be on deck going along the Mersey, past the Point of Ayre, the Mull of Galloway, the Cumbraes and going up the Clyde, but he had been in the habit of going for rest after passing the Mull during good weather. He gave details of a course to take from the Mull and said he would pass within a half or quarter mile of Portpatrick light, steering north and be quite safe. After rounding the Mull he would regard himself safe for two or three hours.

Captain Boyd said he felt entitled to sleep during either of the four-hour watches. He said: "If the vessel run straight by the land, a quarter mile off, there is no danger. He [the second mate] must have run closer, however, and if he did go nearer, I would say I was not responsible, because it would be beyond what I would expect from him, as a thing unreasonable and unsafe." With regards to the lifeboats he said they were rarely examined; eighteen months could go by without them ever being taken down. Captain Boyd did state that if there had been a haze at the Mull it should have led to greater caution. As a regular commander of vessels running the Liverpool/Glasgow station he knew that his own, The Admiral, would make the sailing in three tides but the Orion made it in two, "but it would be very close for her to do it in that time. This running close to the coast was to endeavour to avoid the strength of the current and get out of the way of other vessels. We gained very little, indeed, from avoiding the tide."

The next witness, John Gilmour, the dockmaster at Liverpool, spoke highly of both Captain Henderson and John Williams. Henderson, he said, was a "steady well-behaved man" and the second mate, "a steady man who attended to his duties manfully." Then Captain Crawford of the Princess Royal, who had been at sea for more than forty years took the stand and gave evidence that to a great extent mirrored the experience of Captain Boyd. His vessel could also make the journey in two tides and was second only to the Orion in swiftness. He also would have no hesitation, in fine weather, in retiring and leaving the watch with a second mate with whom he had confidence. The mate was entitled to alter the course and it was up to his discretion to inform the senior officer either when he did it, or when the captain returned on deck.

Captain McKellar, who had served on the same route but was then on the Liverpool/Derry station, and Captain Hardie, the commander of the Admiral, Alexander Clarke, first mate of the Princess Royal, Captain Wheeler of the Fenella, Captain Dalzell, Captain Kelland, John Honeyman and Adam Dowson all appeared in court to give very similar evidence with regard to route, the lifeboats and the routine of the watches. Captain Dalzell, the agent for the underwriters, said that the Orion was the finest of vessels and well kept. He said Henderson was a superior officer and there was no question that he might safely retire when passing the Mull of Galloway in those weather conditions. He said the compasses must be adjusted before the vessel sails but, they may, shortly afterwards, go "slightly wrong" on account of the influence of local attraction. He said he had once been on an iron ship wrecked for this reason off the Norfolk coast.

The Orion's first mate, George Langlands, was then called as a witness. He said: "We left Liverpool at thirty minutes past four. There was a little haze on the Mull of Galloway, we were about three quarters of a mile off, passing the shore. There was nothing in the night to cause the least apprehension. The land was quite clear, the stars were shining." Langlands kept the ships log and read from the entry for the 17th June which began with "calm and hazy" before giving the times for leaving and passing major landmarks. He qualified his description by adding that what he meant was that the horizon was not distinctly visible. "We could see a long way notwithstanding. We saw the Isle of Man, I suppose seven or eight miles off. It was as fine a night as I had seen on that passage." He described how they rounded Dunman Head, which was quite clear, about a half mile off. He said it was the Captain's practice never to put any east into his course when the vessel had rounded this point. It was after passing this headland that Langlands went below.

With regards to the launching of the lifeboats, the first mate gave his clear opinion that the fault lay with the passengers. "There was nothing to prevent the boats being launched if the seamen had had their way; of course it was difficult on account of the crowd of passengers. There was great confusion and alarm. The boats in their chocks were crowded." He added that the captain had kept his composure and done all he could to save lives. He said that in all his sailing experience he had never seen plugs attached to lifeboats. In answer to a question from Mr Penney, he said that whilst it was understood the mate had discretion in giving any course he thought proper on his watch, that was within the proper course generally. "Variations in such a coasting course are always necessary and it is not thought necessary to report them," adding that he had always found Williams a "trustworthy, steady man thoroughly acquainted with the coast." Under questioning from the Solicitor General, Langlands said that he had not heard any comments on their proximity to the coast and there was nothing to "excite apprehension."

He was followed by William Finlay Johnston, clerk to the Orion's owners, who stated that he had been in charge of supervising the recovery of the cargo, accepted that there had been some rod iron brought up from the starboard side, and there had been iron in the form of sheet, plate and nails in the afthold. This was confirmed by Alex Moore who worked for Mr McClure, the purchaser of the wreck.

William Hatchard, who had previously worked with the inventor of the electric telegraph, Mr Cooke, appeared as a witness to explain that he had been asked to make certain experiments by 'parties connected with the ship's owners.' He had made these experiments assisted by Mr Edwin Clark. They had placed several tons of iron, plate, and nails, on different floors to a compass within a building, with everything else removed. They found that 23cwt of iron placed at a distance of 12 feet deflected the compass fully two degrees. Mr Clark agreed that the experiments had been made with the greatest possible care.

Captain Walter Douglas, the marine superintendent with Messrs Burns then gave evidence about the appointment of Captain Henderson who had been chosen from amongst several candidates. He believed that during the nine months he had commanded the Orion, Henderson had proved himself to be the best man for the job. He stated that it was common practice to cover lifeboats to protect them from the weather and the sea and for the plugs to be kept in a locker or stern sheet. Captain Douglas said that all the boats on the Cunard line were kept in the same way. He said that he had approved of the introduction of the spray cloth at the bottom of the boats, which were to protect the steerage passengers and he had not believed they would form any impediment to being launched.

Sailmaker, Andrew Small told the court that he had made the covers for the boats the preceding February and had studied to make the fastenings as easily removable as possible. He said that in an emergency he would cut the fastenings, but if a knife were not to hand then it would take a minute to a minute and a half to manually remove them. He added: "A sailor without a knife would be like a sailor without a blue jacket, he would be of little use."

The next witness, David Croall, had been the carpenter on the Orion from her launch until only two weeks before she sank. He claimed the davits for the lifeboats had been the same under Captain Main, before Captain Henderson took over and his introduction of the spray sheets should not have caused any problem to releasing the lifeboats, they should have just torn away.

The final witness for the defence was the Orion's previous commander, Hugh Main who then took the stand saying he had been a captain of Liverpool steamers for 20 years and knew Williams to be a good seaman, attentive and cautious. He said that on this route he generally kept in shore at about half a mile, depending on the weather, usually passing a mile off Portpatrick and Blackhead. He said that in fine weather and with a second officer in which he had confidence he would take a little rest during a passage.

The conclusion of the defence case was followed by speeches from the counsel. The Solicitor General addressed the Jury on behalf of the Crown and contended that the facts proved established the guilt of the mate who was in charge of the vessel at the time of the accident and the captain had been guilty of the charges laid against him in respect of his having committed the vessel to the care of a subordinate officer, when near the shore, without any necessity for his doing so and was, therefore, answerable for the unskilfulness of the officer to whom, under such circumstances, he had committed her.

The Solicitor General said that it was "scarcely possible to conceive a shipwreck under more painful circumstances. The calmness and stillness of the night, mothers asleep with their children and everyone reposing in the feeling of as much security as if they had been by their own firesides and in a few short moments – within a stone's throw of the shore – fifty of them had gone down to the deep." The jury had to decide firstly was there blame and secondly who was to blame. He also commented that large quantities of iron were shipped daily between Liverpool and Glasgow with no deflection on compasses observable. He instructed the Jury to look carefully at the position of the rock, that it was obvious that even if the vessel had missed it, she would still have struck the cliffs of the shore. He said he would not stop to describe the "fearful and heart-rending scenes which ensued, which were altogether beyond the power of anyone to describe."

The Solicitor General said that "there was a light hung on the Portpatrick pier, which was reported by the look-out; the vessel was rapidly approaching the shore having deviated from her ordinary course by a mile and a half eastward so that the inhabitants of Portpatrick imagined it was a vessel coming into harbour, and though the warning was given, the vessel still steered in its mad career." He added that the vessel had been taken so close to shore to avoid the force of the current in order to gain the tide at Greenock and carry them up to Glasgow. "It was well known how hardened people became by the success of such experiments and there was scarcely a single department of locomotion in which catastrophes of this kind did not occur from time to time, from parties growing confident from these attempts."

The Lord Justice Clerk then intimated to the counsel for the pannels that the court did not intend to direct the Jury that any case had been sufficiently made with respect to the charge regarding the lifeboats. Mr Penney told the Jury that the accident had been occasioned by causes over which Williams had no control and he was not criminally responsible. The deflection of the compass by which he steered were sufficient to account for the orders he gave especially as he had not been given a copy of the ship's manifest or knew the position of the iron in the cargo hold. Mr Penny pleaded: "Do not throw on this man the awful responsibility of having been by his reckless conduct the cause of losing the lives of so many of his fellow creatures. Do not take from that man the character on which he earns his daily bread."

On behalf of the captain, Mr Crauford cited other legal cases to show that a person is not criminally responsible except for his own act, but he had delegated to a competent person and when he had left the deck there was nothing to show that the vessel was in any danger. "The greater the recklessness of the mate in disregarding the intimations of the nearness of the shore went to exoner the captain who could not calculate on such disobedience to his own orders, and of such unskilful seamanship on the part of an officer chosen for that purpose by the company, who was not shewn to have evinced recklessness or unskillfulness on former occasions."

Mr Crauford said that the captain had been "entitled to believe that his directions to keep westwards would be observed, and this the more especially as the coast was more or less visible." He referred to Captain Henderson's bravery in clinging to the top most spar as boatful after boatful of passengers were safely conveyed away while he remained and "when the waves closed over the finest ship that had ever steamed, the captain who had left Liverpool as proud a man who had ever stepped on a quarter deck was the last to leave the last shattered fragment above the seething waters."

The Lord Justice Clerk, in charging the Jury, said that the intention to do wrong was no part of the crime of culpable homicide; if intention was proved under such a charge then it would be murder. He said the crime of culpable homicide was committed whenever a person unintentionally committed an act whereby the life of another was lost, or when he failed to perform his duty when charged with the preservation of life without having a sufficient excuse for such neglect and life was lost as a consequence. He cited the case of Paton and McNab in 1845 – 'that any person placed in a situation in which his acts may affect the safety of others, must take all precautions to guard against the risk to them arising from what he is doing." He said that it was unnecessary for the pannels to be guilty to the same extent. There might be innumerable degrees of guilt incurred under such a charge occasioned by not merely the amount of recklessness displayed but by the amount of duty and responsibility which the party had undertaken. Such an occurrence as that before the Jury where a vessel was shown to have been sailing for a long distance unusually near the shore, and at length, immediately after seeing the Portpatrick Harbour Light continuing the same course until the vessel was struck on a well-known rock, on a calm and comparatively clear night, threw on those on whom her management depended the onus of showing respectively that they had done everything in their power to prevent the occurrence of such a catastrophe.

The Lord Justice Clerk said it was not a relevant defence for the captain to say that the mate had navigated the vessel in a more careless and reckless manner than usual if he, the captain, was not justified in committing her care to the mate at all. He added that on the other hand it was no defence for the mate to say that the captain having improperly committed the ship to his care, he had so completely neglected the charge he had undertaken as, after repeated warnings, to run on shore by a course of reckless navigation whereby the vessel was wrecked and a great loss of life occasioned.

Lord Justice Clerk said that in reference to the captain going to rest it was not answer in law for him to say that others had been in the same practice of committing the like wrong, if the Jury were of the opinion that this had been a neglect of duty. He said: "Nothing could be more mischievous than such a doctrine as it was the occasion of almost all like accidents. Men became accustomed to perils and daily became more and more daring and rash in their exercise of their avocations; and it surely was no answer when at length the danger which had been so often run, resulted in the death of more than fifty beings, to urge that hundreds daily before had been in danger from a course of like reckless conduct. It was much to be feared that captains often ran close to the shore to avoid currents and tides, in order to save time and having escaped disasters on repeated occasions by such courses, they become overconfident and at length adopt a course which at first they would have thought insane to attempt." He told the Jury that the leading principle to be adopted in judging such cases was not "how near to the coast a captain might venture without danger but how far off he ought to be in order to avoid all risk."

The Jury was asked to consider whether the captain was justified in needing rest given the fact that the loading of the cargo was not supervised by him, the steering of the Mersey was by a river pilot, and the voyage normally took no longer than 15 hours. Whilst it had been observed that the course taken was not much different from normal he said: "No doubt companies were anxious to make quick voyages for the sake of profit, and captains were anxious to please their employers by performing the voyage as quickly as possible. Honesty of intention and anxiety to serve the interests of his employers did not form a justification for directing or sanctioning a course so in-shore." Whatever the pressures, the captain's primary duty was to preserve the lives of the passengers who sailed in his ship.

With reference to the mate, his case regarding the deflection of the binnacle compass had "entirely failed." It had been proved, beyond doubt, that land was clearly visible northwards from the Mull of Galloway. Had he called the captain when he perceived they were so close to shore and had he then sanctioned the course they were following, the mate might have been as much relieved as the steersman, who obeyed Williams' orders. But this had not been done.

His Lordship said that with reference to the lifeboats there was not enough evidence to convict on these charges but he commented that if in the future it was found that lives were lost because of an inability to launch because

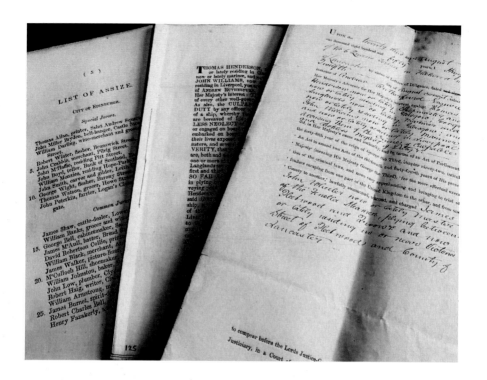

*The Orion trial documents.*

of these coverings and devices there would be grave consequences for any captains or proprietors who failed to supply or maintain the boats for purpose.

The Lord Justice Clerk asserted that if the lifeboats had been sufficiently ready and handy for the purpose of saving life in the event of a sudden shipwreck, and if the plugholes had not been left open with the plugs not to be found, many more lives might have been saved. "It appeared," he said, "that in the merchant service where, of all others, lifeboats are most required it was the practice to have them carried more for ornament than immediate use." He criticised ship owners for their economies that instead made the public suffer, that a pound or two a year would repair any damage from the sun of Scotland or Liverpool, these vessels were not sailing on the coast of Senegal or the river Gambia where they might need protection.

The Lord Justice Clerk said that officers became so familiarised with the voyage that they forgot the risks they ran; they knew the current was less strong along the shore, but they forgot the danger of hugging it too closely. "Such catastrophes generally arise from some one person only doing a very little more than was done before. People get so confident that they become altogether insensible to the danger," he added.

His Lordship commented that the captain had adopted a coasting course in which a vessel might certainly avoid a shipwreck, but it was a course that required "special care, constant attention and skill and watchfulness, more so than if the vessel had been taken out to sea. It was a course full of risk and requiring great skill and yet at this time the captain left the deck."

## The Sentence

The Jury were then invited to retire. After only half an hour they were back in court with their verdicts. They found Captain Thomas Henderson, by a majority, guilty of culpable but not reckless neglect of duty and, unanimously, found John Williams guilty of culpable and reckless neglect of duty. Lord Wood then pronounced the sentence. He said that when the Orion, one of the finest, best equipped vessels in the trade, had set sail with a valuable cargo and more than 200 people on board, that "every man who had charge of her navigation should have had the thought indelibly impressed on his mind that no vigilance, no care, and no anxiety which he could bestow in the navigating of this vessel to the port of her destination, should be awanting." But the contrary was the case. The captain had chosen a coasting course apparently trying what peril he could put the vessel into instead of thinking how best to bring her safely to port. There was a clear, known course that they were accustomed to and she was under the charge of men who knew every part of the voyage. He referred to the calmness and clearness of the night, the tranquillity of the water and the vessel within sight of land – "that the vessel should have struck is a very deplorable and astonishing result."

The Jury had found that it could only have occurred by the reckless and culpable neglect of duty of one or another of the persons in charge of the vessel. In these circumstances, he felt he could do no other than give, in the case of John Williams, a sentence of transportation for seven years, and in the case of Thomas Henderson, imprisonment for eighteen months. Lord Ivory and The Lord Justice Clerk concurred. Lord Wood said that in the case of Captain Henderson he hoped the sentence would have the effect of teaching all those in charge of such vessels, the impressive lesson of the duty that is incumbent on them and the strictest and most watchful and most unceasing vigilance in the navigation of vessels is necessary on these short voyages. "I cannot but believe that if the captain had not neglected his duty and left the deck, that if he had been there exerting the skill he is known to possess, that on this occasion no wreck would have taken place and that the cargo and passengers would have all arrived safe at port instead of fifty of them having been drowned and the lives of all the rest put in danger."

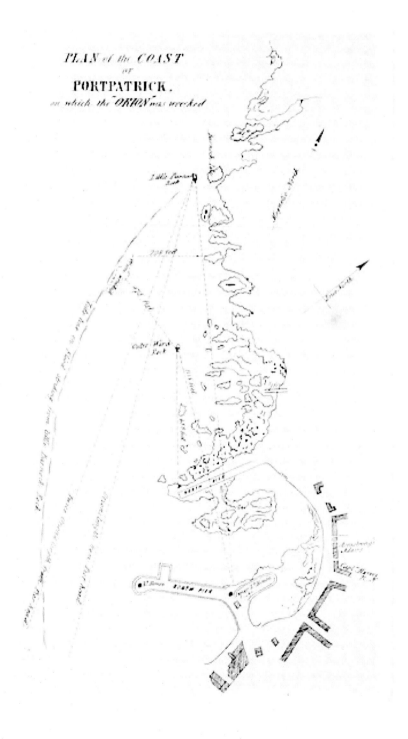

PLAN of the COAST
OF
PORTPATRICK.
on which the ORION was wrecked

# Chapter Eight

*"Something approaching insanity drove
his noble vessel on open destruction. "*

The verdict of the trial was widely reported, there had been great interest nationally in the wrecking of the Orion and the indictment of the three officers. On the 2nd of September, the Shipping and Mercantile Gazette stated: "There can be no question of the justice of this decision especially as it regards Williams. The man would appear to be have been guilty of a wilful and deliberate act of crime rather than ignorance or neglect of duty and it is due to those in command of our Merchant Shipping - whether steamers or sailing vessels – to impress upon the public mind the fact that conduct of this kind – happily a rare occurrence – cannot escape the punishment which it justly deserves."

The *Glasgow Herald* on the same date wrote: "We can only trust that the remembrance of this case will in all time coming, act as a warning against the negligence and over confidence which has produced results so deplorable and calamitous." Many commentators were astonished at the way the Orion had been sailed around the Scottish coast. Captain Gipp Robinson was highly praised for his clear and informed evidence. The North British Daily Mail commented that it was impossible to read his evidence without being convinced of the course the Orion should have steered and that this should be impressed upon all commanders. The captain had stated that a ship taking a N ½ W course from Cromack Point at a distance of half a mile from land would be clear of all danger, but the Orion had been only 200 yards off and her course was repeatedly altered with a view to bring her more and more in shore. The result was that she "grazed Portpatrick pier" whereas she should have been a mile away.

The newspaper declared that the wrecking of the Orion was caused by the "inveterate temerity with which the second mate deviated from the N ½ W course eastward, zig-zagging round the coast." It was also felt that Captain Gipp Robinson had clearly repudiated the idea that a steam ship of the size and power of the Orion could be "materially impeded" by the currents a mile offshore. The Orion's course had been the "result of a mistake, a sheer foolhardy prejudice and ought now to be universally condemned and abandoned." It was generally hoped that the trial would render the safety of passengers a more important object in the eyes of commanders than it had hitherto been. "Speed is the result which all passengers desire, but none wish for it if it is only secured at the hazard of their lives."

The *Greenock Advertiser* devoted a considerable number of its columns to the case on the 3rd of September, understandably given the close connection its readers had to the Orion and the community that served the maritime industry. The editorial began with lines from The Shipwreck by Lord Byron, used at the start of this book. Given the importance of sea travel to the population of an island nation, it is not surprising that the trial of the Orion's officers was regarded as a landmark case, indeed the leader writer believed that it had been the most important to have ever occurred in Scotland at that time.

The author of the editorial had to strike a considered balance given that the owners of the ship were a powerful and influential local company, whilst officers and crew serving on the steamers were also amongst its readers. The industry was highly competitive with many rival companies running ships along the same routes and the tragedy had been a commercial and personal disaster for Messrs Burns, losing a brother and niece along with their star steamer. There was also the impact not only caused by the loss of confidence from the public in their shipping line, but the immediate threat of financial ruin due to possible legal action from insurance companies.

The Cork Examiner had noted in July that the Orion's loss could lead to insurers taking action against Messrs Burns. "Captain McNeill, it is stated, and others of the passengers drowned, had their lives insured for large sums; and an impression prevalent in Glasgow is that an attempt will be made to establish the liability of the steam-boat company, to pay a rateable proportion, according to the value of the different parties' lives at the time of the accident." The writer was unsure of what act the action would be brought under – saying that Lord Campbell's Accident Act did not apply in Scottish law – but this all depended on whether carelessness was proven. During the trial there were repeated references by several different masters, that when commanding the vessels, they were under no rules or instructions to abide by in terms of the companies they worked for, no company policies in terms of course selection. This was, perhaps, in itself, an instruction so that the shipping companies were not liable for any subsequent legal action in terms of passengers' life insurance.

The population of the UK living during this extraordinary period of change that we now call the Industrial Revolution, had seen a transformation in the means of transport in a short time. As one journalist wrote, going from "the slow and infrequent movements" of thousands of travellers 30 years before to millions taking advantage of the enormous breakthroughs in transportation. "Steam locomotion has become the safest of all movements when prudence is not despised but is dangerous beyond calculation when its government is committed to incompetent or careless men." The *Greenock Advertiser* wrote: "Though the punishment in the case of both prisoners is severe and especially so in the case of Captain Henderson, it could not have been of a milder nature on their being declared guilty of the offence by the verdict of the jury. The loss of one of the finest steam vessels which ever floated on the surface of the deep and the consigning, in a moment when danger seemed so remote as to be next to impossible, of fifty human beings to death, were offences of too great a magnitude not to be followed by an amount of punishment which would at least have the effect of deterring others situated in the like circumstances from abandoning their reasoning in imagined security, or to the unwarrantable desire of shortening the duration of the passage by a few minutes at a risk which ought never to be undertaken by any responsible agent. There is not one man to whom the terrible of calamity of the Orion shipwreck is known but will pity the officers of the vessel, especially Captain Henderson; but no one even with the consequences of such a sentence can divest himself of the idea that the severity of the law was required to be decisive and imperative. We live in times when officers of steam vessels and railway engines drivers should be aware that from one end of their route to another a sword is hanging over their heads."

Captain Henderson was described as one of the "ablest and cautious of his profession" but had "to suffer that the masters of ships in the future shall place no confidence in inferior officers, no matter of what steadiness and skill, but at their own peril. Captain Henderson was lying in the twilight of a calm and beautiful summer morning when something approaching insanity drove his noble vessel on open destruction." The writer of the *Greenock Advertiser* did have some words for Williams too, saying that he understood him to be a "sober and clever officer" but his "inexplicable conduct on one fatal night" had brought upon him years of misery and the punishment of his superior officer.

Captain Thomas Henderson came from a wealthy family of master mariners, and, it is clear that the journalists of the *Greenock Advertiser* were being cautious in their reporting of the case. John Williams however did not have the same luxury of privilege or influence. Interestingly, on Scotland's east coast, the reporters of the Dundee Courier carried an article that questioned just how 'superior' an officer Captain Henderson was. A piece that was carried in newspapers as far afield as Buckinghamshire, Cheltenham, and Cork, carried information gleaned from the prison service which shone a different light on the captain.

After the trial, the prisoners were taken to Calton Hill Jail, the remains of which are now known as the Governor's House in Edinburgh and serve as offices for the Scottish Fiscal Commission. They were taken by hackney cab from the High Court, arriving between seven and eight o'clock on the Saturday evening. Williams was described as being in "extreme dejection" submitting in "perfect silence to the usual operation of exchanging his own clothes for the prison dress which consisted of a course suit of dark grey cloth – jacket, trousers and vest and canvas shoes." Prison staff had noted that his conduct since his incarceration had been "exemplary" and had "enlisted sympathies of all who came into contact with him." After the initial shock of his sentence had passed Williams had shown himself to be a mild, civil and "not a little communicative."

*The Courier* wrote: "He states that he had not the slightest idea of danger until the land was seen right ahead when he instantly became aware of the impossibility of escaping it. Nonetheless he immediately ran to the helm and endeavoured to give another direction to the vessel, but the fruitlessness of all efforts to prevent the approaching catastrophe he saw at a glance and the agony of his mental suffering at that moment and ever since has been of the most intense description. He is now much calmer and feels relieved when an opportunity presents itself of giving expression to his feelings of mortified professional skill and of deep regret for the awful catastrophe he occasioned for he fully admits the possibility of his having given an erroneous course to the steersman although that he should have done so is a mystery even to himself."

In contrast, the same source reported a quite different picture of Captain Henderson. "We regret to say he has not conducted himself in so becoming a manner as the inferior officer. He displays more impatience and moroseness than vexation at the severity of his sentence, or the loss of reputation and position in society. The regulations of the prison were enforced, in his case, with as much gentleness as they admit of and a regard for his feelings required; but the painful duty of the officers was rendered still more unpleasant by the ill-considered behaviour of the unfortunate man himself." The reporter added that there had been further particulars of the captain's behaviour, but he felt that this example was enough to show his demeanour. It is likely that the newspaper's legal advisers probably told the journalist to leave the other reports unpublished. After a week at Calton jail the surgeon there signed the necessary medical certificate for the removal of Captain Henderson who was taken on the Perth and Dundee Railway accompanied by three prison officers, to serve his sentence at Perth prison.

This view of Captain Henderson was less of surprise to those fortunate enough to have survived the disaster. Writing his original book not long after the trial had ended, Reverend Joseph Clarke shared his opinion of the man and thoughts expressed by other passengers as they sailed away from Portpatrick on the Princess Royal, the day after the sinking.

One of those on board, accountant William Anderson, whose makeshift clothing included a woman's shawl and night cap, had made no secret of his feelings that there had been "gross and culpable carelessness show. First in striking the rock and next in getting the boats down. The crew seemed paralysed and as helpless as any passengers." Mr Clarke's feelings on the trial were that it had been too focused on whether or not the captain should have been on deck or resting, and who was to blame between the two officers. Many of the passengers felt that there had been a "shutting out of evidence" at the trial, and although many of the survivors were listed as witnesses including Adam Forbes, John Carstairs McNeill, Mary Houston, Archibald McKechnie, as well as Hugh and George Miller, only Elizabeth Colquhoun was called.

It was felt that the captain's conduct after the ship had struck should have been included in the evidence presented to the court. In this matter there were strong views of what a man in command of a vessel should have done in terms of lowering the boats and attempting to save the lives of those committed to his care. Many believed that Captain Henderson should have been present from the first to supervise the boats and to insist on women and children being taken first. "We have little doubt," Mr Clarke wrote, "had this been done – not a tenth part of those, who now are no more, would then have met with a watery grave." Instead the captain had not been found immediately and then was heard, contrary to the evidence of one crewmate, assuring the panicking throng that the ship would not sink.

An excellent article written in 2010 for the Liverpool Nautical Research Society by Gordon Bodey draws on several sources that presented a view of the captain's actions that were contrary to how the master had been presented in court. Mr Bodey wrote that the captain "had been asleep below rather than on deck during most of the passage along the Galloway peninsula (which, on its west side, is for almost its whole length bounded by very precipitous cliffs and jagged rocky outcrops) after Ardwell Point, and when roused came on deck in his 'shirt and drawers' by the account of the Rev. George Thomson. Climbing onto a seat he shouted to the passengers, 'Keep to the ship - you are all safe if you keep to the ship.' To a man who said to him that the ship was quite near the shore, Captain Henderson said, 'We are too near the shore, that has been the cause of it.'

He told the ladies to compose themselves claiming this was 'no occasion for alarm,' whereupon one of them pointed out to him that the ship was already listing badly and that the main cabin deck was awash. Shortly afterwards he was observed near the engine-house shouting that there was no danger and to keep calm, apparently under the impression that the ship would settle on the rock she had struck and remain above water. However, this was not to be as the vessel had rebounded after the impact and slid off the rock, probably helped by the southward flow of the tide (which commences its southward flow two hours before low water), and soon heeled over so badly that it was not possible to stand upright without a handhold.

Steerage passenger, Mr Adam Forbes a bookbinder of Stirling, later stated that he also saw the captain in his shirt and drawers standing near the engine-house shouting out that there was no danger, and to keep calm. He also said that a large number of passengers at first agreed with the captain's initial opposition to the launch of the lifeboats - the captain calling on all to remain with the ship saying that there was no danger and threatening to, 'cut the hands off the first man that should touch the boats.' A cabin passenger, Peter Townsend, an accountant of Sherwood Street, Liverpool, also attested to the master's state of undress and his appearance of having just got out of bed, and to his reluctance to have the boats launched. Mr. Townsend was ordered out of a boat that he was helping to clear by the master. Donald McKinnon also attested (two weeks later at Fort William) that he heard the master calling on everyone to stand by the ship and that he had delayed ordering the boats to be lowered." -1

Away from the trial there was good news and an outpouring of generosity from the surviving passengers of the Orion. A meeting was held in Glasgow in September to organise a subscription for the Portpatrick boatmen. A committee was appointed, and subscriptions invited from passengers from all over the country, varying from £1 to £10. It was acknowledged that many people had privately rewarded members of the community who had provided their homes, clothing, and support to the survivors and the bereaved. Many of the subscribers attended a further meeting on the 28th November at the Religious Institution Rooms in Glasgow when the treasurer Mr Thomas Kidston announced that £203 (£27,550 today) had been raised, mainly in the city. With the help and advice of Captain Hawes, Reverends Urquhart and Balmer and Dr Robertson, the treasurer and Mr Thomson from the committee were asked to travel to Portpatrick to distribute the money. Free rail tickets were provided to and from Ayr by the chair of the Ayrshire Railway Company, and free passage on the steamer Scotia from Ayr to Stranraer.

In Portpatrick the two men were asked to investigate and classify the claims of people in the village and decide whether they would best benefit from a gift of money or something useful to them like blankets, clothing, payment of debts, fishing lines etc. The sum of £6 was presented to each person who had saved lives. An order was made for a new boat to be built for two of the most expert and daring of the fishermen, brothers James and John Crawford, and they were so delighted with this news that they had resolved to call the boat the Orion, when she was launched. Dr Robertson and Captain Hawes declined any reward, though the doctor was presented with a silver snuff box as a memento of their gratitude.

Mr Thomson addressed the gathering when the money and goods were distributed. "The public, by their willing liberality, wish not only to reward you, but to show to the fishermen and to others around our coasts, that they are as ready to reward disinterested conduct such as yours, as they are to abhor the inhumanity of those who, on such occasions, disregarding alike the voices of their own conscience, and the cry of their helpless fellow creatures, think only of plunder and bring reproach and shame on themselves and shame on our country, may the hated name of wrecker never more be heard on our coasts. We here who are saved from the wreck can bear willing testimony to your disinterested and valuable efforts on that fearful morning, and not only you the boatmen, but the whole population of Portpatrick, young and old, as if animated by one noble spirit of benevolence and kindness, sought only how they could succour, comfort and animate their weak and almost naked fellow creatures, so suddenly and fearfully thrown upon their kindness. But if we may judge your characters by your conduct of that time, the satisfaction of your own minds, and the universal commendations which we can assure you have been bestowed on the whole people of Portpatrick, must be more highly prized by you than any other rewards that may have been bestowed upon you."

This sense of community pride and celebration was, tragically, marred by the deaths of two of the main recipients only a month later. The two brothers whose bravery in saving so many lives from the wreck and who had been rewarded with the commissioning of a new boat that they planned to call Orion, were themselves, drowned. On Hogmanay 1850 three fishermen 23-year old James Crawford and his 17-year-old brother John, and friend James Gordon left Portpatrick in a small boat to lift their fishing lines. After they left the harbour a wind came up, blowing hard and in attempting to put into Larbrax Bay a wave had struck the boat broadside and it had immediately capsized. James Gordon managed to swim to shore and alerted local farmer Charles Kerr who, along with others, immediately returned with him to the beach. James Crawford was pulled ashore but "unhappily life was extinct." Mr Kerr had despatched a boy immediately to Portpatrick to fetch Dr Robertson but sadly when he arrived at the scene, he was unable to revive the man. It was thought that John Crawford had become entangled in the fishing lines and at the time of the report – 8th January 1851 – the *Dumfries and Galloway Standard* said that his body had not been found.

Another curious story connected to the tragedy that had befallen the McNeill family made the news shortly after the trial. It transpired that earlier in the year Captain McNeill had commissioned the building of a "handsome mausoleum" on a prominent rock on the Isle of Gigha, which he owned. He wished the building to be of a sufficient size to entomb six people, but the architect had reported that owing to the limitations of the site, the design could not contain more than four and this suggestion was accordingly adopted. This structure had only just been completed when the Orion was wrecked, and "in that receptacle of the dead are now deposited the remains of the gallant captain and the three members of his hapless family who perished with him."

*The Orion at low water.*

# Chapter Nine

*"For the sake of saving half an hour, the ship and her living cargo were gratuitously exposed to perils wholly independent of the ordinary dangers of the deep."*

The horror and disbelief felt by those Portpatrick people as they witnessed the Orion, the pride of the fleet, steaming at full throttle towards the rocks north of the village was echoed throughout the country as the news of the wrecking was relayed in the days that followed. The reporters of the London Evening Mail on the 3rd July wrote the words so many were repeating to each other – the Orion had no business to be within many hundreds of yards of the rocks. A sketch (below) drawn up for the Glasgow newspaper the *Reformers' Gazette* on the 6th July illustrated that the Orion was being steered out of her usual and regular course. "Any person with ordinary observation will see that the Orion was at least one mile off her course for no ship would dare sale closer to such a shore as this than one mile, especially when there is a tide running sometimes at a rate of two and a half to three knots an hour." This was the first newspaper to mention that there had been some initial claims that there was a channel between the rock and the land but this was not the case, and anyway it was clear that even had she missed the rocks, she was headed straight for the cliffs ahead.

The *Dumfries and Galloway Standard* wrote a hard-hitting piece about the impact of such a tragedy. "It is not a simple feeling of sorrow, however deep, that is aroused, but mingling with it there is a sterner emotion, a sense

Map of the route of the Orion.

of indignation such as one feels when some deed of heartless and wanton cruelty has been inflicted on a crowd of innocent and unsuspecting victims. The Orion tragedy possesses elements peculiar to itself - such as separate it widely from the countless casualties occasioned in a stormy sea.

"The Orion did not encounter the enmity of the ocean; its waves, at the period of the catastrophe, did not rise in fury against the doomed ship, but bore her peacefully along. Both wind and sea were calm - there was a mellowed moonlight on the bosom of the deep, and day-light was beginning to dawn upon it - all nature was tranquil and serene - and at such a season the devoted vessel was, as it were, decoyed out of her course, and impelled to run upon destruction, and take down with her into the yawning waters the rich argosy of human life committed to her care, and which, but for some unaccountable counteracting agency, she would have borne safely to her destined haven. It is this seeming recklessness or infatuation, sheer obtuseness and stupidity, which excites the mind in perusing the narrative of the wreck.

"The vessel had gone between Liverpool and Glasgow hundreds of times before, and the channel must have been perfectly familiar to her officers. Had the night been a December one, and without a star, their departure from the familiar track would scarcely have been excusable; but to wander many miles out of it, away on the smooth unimpeded sea, into the proximity of an iron-bound coast, and thus causelessly to leave the safe and common course for one in which dangerous rocks were sure to be encountered, was procedure so strange that we cannot find words properly to characterise it. When the noble ship was completely and nearly as suddenly disabled as if she had been rent by a thunderbolt, where were the boats, to which the two hundred startled passengers and crew might have betaken themselves, and rowed to the firm land which lay within a stone's cast. They were tied in such a complicated way to the ship, that it was with the utmost difficulty their fastenings were uncoiled. Had the wreck not been seen from the land, and numerous boats not put off for it, the loss of life would in all likelihood have been doubled at least; under all the circumstances of the case, it is wonderful that so many as a hundred and fifty or more escaped, no life-preservers, save one, having been on hoard, and the boats being too few in number, so difficult to get launched, and so comparatively useless in time of need."

It is impossible to know, and no explanation was ever given, other than to avoid the  current, as to why the Orion was so far from a safe course, but for some months it will have been a topic of theory and conjecture by people in their parlours, offices, public houses and clubs not only in the UK but in other parts of the world. The complacency of hardened men, an opinion stated at the trial, must surely have been a factor, but one wonders to what extent the pressure of competition, and rivalry between steamers were also among the driving forces. These were highly experienced sailors in charge of the swiftest vessel sailing the coastal waters, and one cannot help but consider whether there was pressure from the owners to maintain a speedy reliable service, or how much of this horrifying mistake was driven by personal pride on the part of Captain Henderson. In one of the first reports on the disaster the *Glasgow Herald* speculated: "It would pain us to learn that the prevailing mania for rapid traveling, for we can call it by no other name, had resulted so fatally. There was not as much wind as would have whelmed a child's toy ship nor as much motion in the sea as would have endangered a regatta."

In evidence given at the trial it was stated that the Princess Royal was hard on the heels of the Orion in terms of speed. The advertisements for the various sailings and ships included the names of their captain; there was prestige and status in being a commander, so perhaps there was equally a professional rivalry between the masters. The *Glasgow Herald* again, after the trial, stated: "The motive for this act of temerity appears to have been the lessening of the voyage by an hour or two—not, we presume, in order accommodate the passengers, but to increase the ship's reputation as a fast sailer. When the Orion was thus run out of the usual track she was under the management the second mate; but cannot think that by this account the captain was absolved from responsibility, that he could by any pretence delegate the trust committed to him, and consign over any one the charge of the two hundred precious souls who had embarked in the Orion relying upon his qualifications as her commander."

Whilst it is understandable that there were measures to keep the lifeboats stable during sailings, the chocks, coverings etc, there was obviously an emphasis on presentation rather than their purpose. When they were finally needed to save lives all the various contraptions of cloths, canvases, bolts and strappings meant that it was almost impossible to free them in the horrendously short time between the ship hitting the rock and sinking. The four boats had the capacity to carry all the passengers safely to shore but only one made it successfully into the water and due to a lack of a bung, and oars it was almost like the vessel used by the Jumblies in Edward Lear's children's rhyme – they went to sea in a sieve. The situation was further hampered by the captain's resistance to the disaster unfolding before his eyes. Whilst many of the crew behaved gallantly, others less so and the fact that the vast majority survived speaks volumes. The only ones to perish were the steward, who attempted to save the fares given to him by the steerage passengers and died from the strain and exhaustion of swimming to the shore carrying them, the carpenter who had badly injured himself with his axe while trying to free the lifeboats, and one of the young apprentices.

Instead of the women and children being the first to be saved, they were instead the first to drown. Mothers with young children, if they had cabins, will have been among those, like the Reverend Clarke, who retired early to their bunks and were sound asleep when the accident happened, delaying their ability to gather their thoughts if they even had that opportunity. The evidence of many was that the cabins were knee deep in water by the time they awoke, such was the damage to the ship and the speed with which the water flooded in. Women were then at a further disadvantage due to the social niceties of Victorian society when assessing the risk of danger compared to the thought of leaving the cabin in a state of undress.

Newspaper articles and witness statements frequently referred with shock to the nudity of the survivors, to bare shouldered women saved in just their night attire. The situation will have been, if possible, worse for the steerage women and children given the elaborate skirts, fitted bodices, and petticoats that were standard clothing in 1850. For those that were clothed or attempted to dress there was little chance of survival in the water wearing yards of material and elaborate undergarments, even if they had been able to swim.

The women on the Orion were put in increased danger by the man who should have been doing his utmost to save their lives. Captain Henderson had appeared and entreated them to compose themselves saying there was no occasion for alarm. Thankfully one woman spoke out and questioned his judgement of the situation by pointing out that the ship was listing badly, and water was already making its way into the cabins. Other women acted bravely, a Mrs Napier was reported as having displayed a "remarkable presence of mind, twisting a rope round her waist, she sprang into the sea, caught hold of a plank, then cast off the rope and succeeded in getting hold of a lifebuoy to which she clung with her chin and elbow till relieved by one of the boats, which was a very long time, nearly an hour." One writer even went as far as saying that "it would appear that the terrible scene brought out the female character more favourably than that of the opposite sex; the former appearing more ready to assist each other without regard to personal safety."

Gender and class were important factors in survival and in death. At the beginning of the trial the names of the drowned were very solemnly read out as part of the indictment, a reminder to the officers of those who had perished because of their neglect. But these were inevitably mainly the cabin passengers as no record was kept of the steerage travellers, many were buried unclaimed, and without knowing these numbers the true death toll was never exactly established. Time and again the newspaper articles inevitably focussed on the tragedy of the loss of the wealthier, named cabin passengers and how much of their money and expensive belongings had also been taken to the bottom of the sea. Whilst the equal tragedy of the unnamed, the unknown and uncollected was perhaps felt to be of less interest.

The Victorians were a society obsessed and ruled by their notions of class and, again, one wonders how much this came into play in terms of who took the blame for the Orion's loss. Whilst the captain being below deck brought a great deal of criticism from other commanders, the court and the leader writers, it was the main argument given by his counsel absolving him of any blame, and although the fact that he was found guilty by the jury obviously meant that this was not accepted as a justifiable reason for his plea of not guilty, nevertheless the weight of guilt was placed on the shoulders of the lesser officer. Captain Henderson, despite being the master of the vessel, firmly believed that he was not in any way to blame for the ship's disastrous course although it was confirmed by several members of crew, and experienced sailors travelling as passengers, that the Orion was already sailing closer to the coast while he was still on deck. Who knows what factors came into play here, and what really happened? The captain was seen to look at the compass and speak to Williams before going below. Were all the officers trying to maintain the Orion's reputation for speed, or even, perhaps, set a new record?

John Kelly said in court that they had been "alongside Portpatrick sooner than the usual run." The conditions were probably perfect for trying to cut a few minutes from the journey, to ensure that they caught the tide that would carry them up the Clyde. It seems impossible to believe that Williams, a highly experienced reliable man, would ignore the repeated warnings of the lookouts, and the evidence of his own eyes to try and beat the tide just for his own reasons. Complacency and arrogance were clearly factors. Although there were two men on look-out, passengers stated that shortly before the crash they only saw one, and the sailor who was picked up by the mail coach told the Miller brothers that he had been on watch but was smoking behind the funnel at the time of the collision. But such small mistakes, borne out of habit and routine, do not explain the fact that the Orion was so far off her usual route?

*The Huddersfield Chronicle* published a powerful condemnation of what they considered to be some of the driving forces behind accidents like the wrecking of the Orion. "It is not probable that the owners of the Orion gave specific orders for the destruction of their vessel, or that her commander deliberately resolved on an act of professional immolation, so it becomes important to ascertain what were the causes which operated with effects so exactly analogous to those of wilful and predetermined suicide.

"The cause seems to have been an over anxiety to hug the land, so as to escape the adverse tide and secure a rapid passage. In other words, for the sake of saving half an hour, the ship and her living cargo were gratuitously exposed to perils wholly independent of the ordinary dangers of the deep. With a good vessel, a vigilant commander, and a competent crew, the risks of a sea voyage from Liverpool to Glasgow on such a night as that of the 17th were absolutely inappreciable. The Orion created her own sea risks and met the consequences. Against such temptations as those to which we refer a twofold security is presumed to reside — first, in the true interests of the proprietors and officers of the vessel; and, secondly in the interests of the public. A hundred successful experiments could not compensate the company for the loss of a ship. The captain, in evading or transgressing a seaman's duties, exposes his own life no less than those of his passengers.

"It is thought very desirable that their vessels should have a character for quick passages, and it is clearly expedient that the cargo should be as large as possible. To compass both these results in their fullest shape, a succession of risks is incessantly incurred. Hazardous tracks are taken to save half an hour, and the capacity of the vessel, rather than its capability, is taken to determine the limit of her load. As to the officers, when it comes to the last, life is doubtless as sweet to them as to others; but long habit, frequent escapes, and a spirit of professional rivalry, beget in them a kind of insensate folly which is scarcely credible. What responsibility then can be devised to preclude this wanton exposure of life, how are we to create in proprietors and officers an interest strong enough to deter them from endangering every soul under their care for the sake of seven minutes and a half in a 15 hours voyage, or 50 shillings in the balance of the day's account.

"It can only be by stringent legislation and unsparing example. At present, we may really say, in general terms, that the paramount object of the commander is not the safety of the vessel under his charge. In fact, he rarely gives a thought to this point. His care is how to make a quick passage, to outstrip some rival, and to render the whole speculation remunerative to his employers. He has no more idea of losing his vessel than a cabman of losing his wheel. What he looks to is a rapid drive and a heavy fare. It may be urged, perhaps, that if ship owners, seamen, and passengers, are all thus consenting parties to the risk, it is nobody's business to interfere; but fools and idiots, not to mention women and children, have claims to public protection. Lives are not to be sacrificed to folly or avarice without protest on the part of public censors or intervention on the part of authority."

More than 50 lives had been sacrificed as the crew of the Orion attempted to shave a few minutes off their run, determined to beat the tide so that they would be carried along from Greenock to Glasgow. But was another man's future also sacrificed in the story of the Orion? John Williams, in his mid-fifties, was the much older man, getting towards the end of his career compared with Henderson, age 30, and 26-year-old Langlands. Thomas Henderson not only had the expectation of a glittering and prosperous career ahead, but he also had the considerable influence of his wealth, and background behind him. From his behaviour after his sentence, one that was considerable lighter compared with the seven years of transportation, a severe and hazardous punishment, given to Williams, it seems that Henderson had every reason to believe that he would not be found guilty. Did the officers come to some kind of agreement, with the older man persuaded to take the blame for all their actions, but at the same time hopeful that any fault proven in the compasses would be enough to absolve him? Although the charges were removed against Langlands because he had been below deck for some time before the collision, one of the crew on the first mate's watch had said that he believed they were closer to the Mull than usual when they passed. Given the perfect sailing conditions were all three officers attempting a record time, an attempt that ultimately cost the lives of so many – the vast majority passengers?

Whether the Orion's crew were acting out of loyalty or fear for their future employment, the fact that many, including George Langlands, blamed the panicking passengers for their own fate seems particularly distasteful, especially when almost all of them survived. Time and again survivors disputed the initial claim of the first mate that the deaths were due to the passengers crowding the lifeboats and that all would have been saved if the crushing had not caused the boats to capsize. Mr Deuchers categorically stated in the Liverpool Times that there was no truth in the claim: "All would not have been saved, because the boats would have have been able to carry all the passengers at once, and the vessel sank before they could have returned from shore."

The only three crew to die were a very young apprentice boy, the carpenter who had badly injured himself trying to release the boats, and the long-serving senior steward who swam to shore attempting to save the money from the steerage passengers. As has been seen some sailors acted with great bravery and consideration, like the carpenter and the cook. Yet the statements of others that the commander's behaviour was contrary to what was witnessed and reported by most of the survivors surely indicates that someone's reputation was being protected, or perhaps future careers. When the ship took only fifteen minutes to sink, Captain Henderson's failure to be immediately on the scene, followed by his failure to act decisively and, in fact, to block the attempts by some to free the lifeboats, must have cost the lives of many people.

In a later statement one passenger believed that the captain had possibly been attempting to calm everyone, as a man in his position should, whilst still urging his crew to prepare the boats – but this one voice was contrary to countless other stories from survivors. This evidence was not provided or sought for in court despite many leader writers asking what had happened in those first few minutes, why had the crew been apparently largely inactive when every second counted and, most importantly, why was the alarm not raised on the ship; the Orion's bell was never rung even as the land loomed before them. Many of the passengers died in their berths still asleep or attempting to dress understandably not fully aware of just how much danger they were in. Interestingly according to Gordon Bodey, "on the morning of the disaster, and before he left for Troon, George Langlands, possibly believing that he might eventually have to face a charge with respect to the unseaworthiness of the lifeboats, had the entire remains of the boats carted away to Glasgow." But was he acting on his own initiative? Or had this also been on the orders of his commander who had instructed him to take letters to Glasgow giving his version of what had happened. One cannot help but wonder at what passed between the captain and his first mate after being rescued from the mast, observed by one exhausted survivor to be talking in low voices to each other.

Whilst the families of those that were lost mourned for their loved ones, the nine Smith children in Montreal who had already lost their father and whose mother failed to return from her trip across the Atlantic, or the sons and daughter of John Splatt who had spent years trying to persuade their parents and siblings to join them in Australia; Captain Henderson, according to reports, was mainly concerned with how wronged he felt at being found guilty. The *Glasgow Herald* had echoed the thoughts of many after the trial, though, that "whatever may have been the mistake criminality of Williams, the Jury could not, judging from the evidence, condemn him and at the same time acquit Captain Henderson, who, we repeat, was the party chiefly responsible for the safety of the ship."

Both Henderson and Williams served their sentences, there was no court of appeal in 1850, but their futures would be quite different. Unfortunately, I have not been able, at the point of writing, to find out what happened to John Williams, where he was sent to serve his sentence and if, indeed, he survived, only the reports of his remorse and bewilderment at what had happened. As he was a married man with children his sentence will have had a huge impact not only on him but his dependents.

Thomas Henderson, however, continued to feel aggrieved at his sentence. There was some feeling, from those that sympathised with his predicament, that his employers, the powerful Burns brothers, had been looking for some kind of vengeance for their losses, both in business terms but mainly for their personal losses. G & J Burns were not only ship owners but also the 'de facto' management and financial backers of the Cunard line. Thomas Henderson came out of his imprisonment with his own agenda and very quickly, due to the advantage of having family wealth, re-established himself in the shipping industry.

According to one report, on release from prison he was "put in command of a sailing vessel headed for New York provided by his relatives and friends. The venture was successful." He joined the Handyside brothers who had been shipbrokers and merchants in Glasgow for many years, to oversee international brokerage. In 1855 he became a full partner in the business and Handysides & Henderson was formed.

With backing from his brothers, he went on to establish the famous Anchor Line of steamships. Although due to early losses, the company gained a 'doubtful reputation' at first, it soon began to prosper with further investment from the Henderson family. In his book Scotland and the Sea, author Nick Robins ponders the question: "Did his drive come from giving the Burns family 'one in the eye'?" as the Anchor Line set itself up in direct competition with the Cunard Steamship Company.

When Nicol and Robert Handyside retired, Thomas Henderson's brothers, John, David, and William all joined the business. In 1865 the Anchor Line, under the name Henderson Brothers, opened an office in New York and sold tickets through more than 3000 outlets in North America, later also opening offices in Londonderry, Dundee, and Liverpool. The Anchor Line grew from modest beginnings to become one of the largest mercantile fleets in the world. Forever known as 'Captain Tom' he also served as the chairman of the Lighthouse Commissioners and was a member of the Clyde Navigational Trust. Captain Thomas Henderson died in 1895 after a long, prosperous, and successful career. None of the many references to him and his lifetime of achievement on numerous internet websites include any mention to his also having been the commander of the Orion and the appalling tragedy that happened while he was the master.

WRECK OF THE "ORION," AT HIGH WATER.

*Wreck of The Orion at low water.*

# Survivors' Stories

This section includes a selection of witness accounts given by passengers who survived the sinking of the Orion, to newspapers at the time. I have drawn on many of these reports earlier in the book but I thought some readers may wish to read the accounts in full.

## Perthshire Constitutional Journal June 26th, 1850.
*William Crichton*

We have been indebted to Mr. William Crichton, High Street, Perth for a few particulars connected with his escape from the wreck of the unfortunate vessel. Mr Crichton was on his way home from the United States, from which he recently sailed by the Europa steamer, and upon his safe arrival at Liverpool, was naturally congratulating himself upon his escape from the perils of the deep, little imagining the dire catastrophe that was impending. He states, that after retiring to his berth, which was one of the upper row, he fell asleep, and awoke about one in the morning. He then took off his stockings, which he left on when he lay down, and was dozing over again, when he was roused by the steamer striking upon the rock. It did not occur to him at first that there was any particular danger, but when he looked out he saw that the water was rushing in at the door in a torrent, and that it had already reached the lower berths. He then put on some clothes, and went upon deck, where great confusion prevailed, and great delay and difficulty were experienced in the attempts made to unloose and rig out the boats belonging to the steamer. The passengers were fully as active as the crew in their exertions, but owing to the numbers of people who crowded into the boats, and hung upon them even before they were launched, two of them capsized into the water, and a third had nearly shared the same fate. Mr. Crichton, seeing that there was no deliverance to be expected in this quarter, rather looked round for some other means of safety, and as by this time the steamer had begun rapidly to settle down, he made an attempt to get hold of one of the numerous trunks floating about, but it eluded his grasp, and he went down below the water. Upon again emerging, he found himself providentially close beside a rope, connected with one of the masts. Of this he managed to get hold and wrought himself clear of the water. The captain and another gentleman were above him upon the rope, and there were several females below, who were able to do no more than keep themselves from being submerged. Luckily, they were all eventually got off in safety by the boats belonging to Portpatrick. Mr. Crichton himself was rescued by Dr. Douglas of Portpatrick, whose exertions, both in saving the passengers from the wreck, and in ministering to their needs afterwards, are described as being beyond all praise. He took Mr. Crichton to his house, put him in his own bed, and by dint of restorative applications, succeeded in about an hour in bringing back the natural degree of heat to his body. He also kindly wrote to Mr Crichton's family, apprising them of his safety, but owing to the delay in the Post-office, Mr. Crichton himself forestalled the letter, and was the first to announce to his relatives both his danger and escape. He left Portpatrick by the Princess Royal steamer, which was sent from Liverpool to the assistance of the passengers and he arrived in Perth on Wednesday night. Although not speaking from personal knowledge of the track pursued by the steamers from Liverpool to Glasgow, he states it as the general saying in Portpatrick that the Orion was several miles out of her course, and that the disaster must have been caused by culpable negligence in some quarter. The description which Mr. Crichton gives of the scene on board the Orion, both when the boats were swamped and when the vessel herself was going down, is heartrending and tragic in the extreme. From the position which he occupied, he could see numbers sinking around him on every side, without any possibility of rendering them assistance. Many appeared to be paralysed by the suddenness and extent of the catastrophe, and husbands and wives went down in each other's arms as if resolved to perish together. A great many were 'swept off the deck by the vessel heeling over to the one side, and the numbers thus huddled together presented one another from making any efforts to escape. Mr. Crichton states that there were a great number of trunks and other packages upon deck, which were drifted out to sea, and afterwards secured by the boats, and he himself has been fortunate in recovering a good deal of his property. By a letter he has lately received from Dr. Douglas, it appears that on Friday, the second mate who had charge of the vessel when she struck, has been taken into custody.

## North British Daily Mail Thursday June 20th 1850.
*Escape of Lady Passenger*

Shortly before the vessel struck, she was on the main deck, and she is perfectly satisfied, that at the time, there was no appearance of fog. Immediately after the rock was struck, she ran down to the cabin and found the ladies leaping from their beds in a state of greatest consternation. She had, at a previous period of the evening, advised those with whom she had occasion to be brought into contact, not to undress in retiring but, in the great majority of instances, her advice had been disregarded. However, there was evidently no time to be lost, and the ladies prepared just as they were to go on deck. The captain now appeared and entreated them to compose themselves as there was no occasion for alarm, but our informant at once gave positive assurance to the contrary, by declaring that she had seen the vessel settling down at the bows, and ample proof of the melancholy proof was soon afforded by the water making its way along the cabin floor. The panic which ensued, it is impossible to describe, and much more so was the scene which took place immediately afterwards on the deck. Some persons were praying, others uttering imprecations, others screaming. The lady in question succeeded getting into the first boat that was launched but it was almost immediately swamped. By some means of other she got hold of the helm of the steamer, but she had the greatest difficulty maintaining her position. The vessel was swayed from one side to the other by people rushing in a body to secure a place on the boats. Ultimately an end was put to this tumultuous and painful scene by the vessel gradually sinking beneath the surface, namely first forward and then in the afterpart. Our informant was dragged repeatedly under water, and this combined with her previous exhaustion, rendered her almost unconscious so that she has no idea what for some time followed. However, when she came again to herself, she found that she had secured hold of a rope attached to the upper portion of the rigging and fortunately she also observed a cushion floating past her, which she likewise seized hold of. With this she experienced no difficulty in supporting herself and she regained her composure. For some time, she imagined that she would never reach the shore, but as time wore on she got rid of her fears and latterly looked forward to being rescued with some confidence. She remained hanging by the rope for three quarters of an hour and at the end of that time she was picked up by one of the boats. She was landed in a state of great exhaustion but ultimately was able to recover with the effect that she proceeded her [to Glasgow] with the Princess Royal.

One survivor was deliberately dressing himself in the state room after the vessel had struck, not anticipating any immediate danger, when his attention was aroused by hearing a trickling noise like water falling. His first impression was that the induction tap of the wash hand basin table, which stood in the middle of the floor, had been left open and overflowed; but on closer scrutiny he found to his horror that water was welling and rushing up through the waste pipe in the bottom of the basin and pouring over. The ship had already sunk so deep in the water that the sea was forcing its way into the cabin through the basin. He took the hint, did not wait to finish his toilet, and escaped by a miracle.

Mr Deuchars of Liverpool: At the time when the vessel struck I do not believe theMr Deuchars of Liverpool: At the time when the vessel struck I do not believe there was a single person on deck. The sea was smooth as glass; it was a perfect calm, and there was not the least fog. The Orion struck on a rock exactly at the entrance Portpatrick, not fifty yards from the entrance to the port, and not one hundred yards from the lighthouse. Almost immediately after she struck the ship's bow began to settle down, and her stern was raised high the air, and she went down this way. When I rushed on deck, I found wife and child there before me. The scene was the most terrible I ever looked at. A number of parties had got into the boats, suspended from the davits, but owing to the fulness of the passengers engaged in getting out these boats, the ropes at one end only were cut, and the boat came stern on into the water, her bow being still held fast, and the parties who were in her precipitated into the sea. The other ropes were subsequently severed, and the boat fell into the water, and turned bottom up. Many passengers sprung on to the bottom of the boat and were kept afloat until boats from the shore came to their assistance. Some of the parties who were thrown into the sea were saved, others were drowned. The other boat was capsized, through similar mismanagement I believe. A very long time elapsed before the lifeboats could be launched, and the vessel was going down rapidly when they were got afloat. Just as the vessel was about to go down, I jumped into one of the boats with my child, and my wife clung to the rigging and was saved. She was one of the last brought on shore. Before I got ashore the Orion was completely under water, but about one fourth of her masts and funnel could be seen above water. She was sitting upright. I did not see the captain, the mate, or the engineer, on deck, nor did I see the crew exerting themselves saving the people as much as they ought to have done. There was no truth in the report which the mate had put through the Daily Mail. He said all hands would have been saved only for the crushing, which caused the boats to capsize. All would not have been saved, because the boats would not be able to carry away all the passengers at once, and the vessel sank before they could have returned from the shore.

Mr George Thomson of Ingram Street, Glasgow: "It was about half-past one that I was awoke by hearing and feeling a strange tearing sort of noise, as if some strong paper was torn. It was so gentle that I thought little of it, and remained in bed, although all the other passengers in the cabin started at once to their feet and rushed on deck. After a very brief interval, one of my neighbours returned, and began with great trepidation to dress. I then apprehended danger, and jumped out of bed, and drawing on my trousers, went on deck, calling at the ladies' cabin, in passing, to tell my wife that she had better get up and dress, although there might not be any immediate danger. " On getting to the quarter-deck, I found a large number of the passengers assembled in great alarm. The vessel, by this time, had settled somewhat by the head, and was lurching over a little to starboard—that is, towards the land. I instantly went below to hasten my wife with her toilet, and put on a little more dress, and sought for a small trunk I had, and brought it to the middle of the floor. "My wife and I now went on deck, and as the vessel was dipping deeper and deeper into the water, I calmly told her that I feared there was little hope, but that we would use every effort to save ourselves. By this time, the water was over the bulwarks at the bow, and the heel of the deck was becoming greater and greater. I then feared that all was over, and clasping my wife to my breast, we both felt resigned to our fate. We then proceeded, at my wife's suggestion, to the stern of the vessel at the larboard side, and as the inclination of the deck became so great as to prevent our standing, I laid hold of one of the belaying pins, and placing my wife between my breast and the bulwark, I there held on. A lady at this moment had got hold of my wife's shawl; but as it was not fastened at the throat, it soon dropped off, and the unfortunate creature slid down the deck into the sea, which was gradually creeping up over the deck as the ship sank. Turning round, I found the whole space within the bulwarks and up to nearly the centre line of the deck filled with a struggling multitude in the gurgling and seething waters; and most of these, I fear, were very soon drowned. As soon as the water reached the companion, the pent air in the cabin forced off the skylights with a most horrid crash, and in an instant after, we were under water, sucked down in the vortex of the sinking ship. When below the surface, I lost hold of my wife, but striking out, found myself above water, and in contact with one of the stays of the mizzen-mast, which I laid hold of at once. I had hardly done so, when my wife rose also to the surface, and I, at once, took her hand and caused her to hold on by the same rope. I placed my legs round the rope, the better to secure my hold, and told her to rest herself on my knee, which she did. " As soon as we had so far secured ourselves, the ship gave a heavy lurch to starboard, which immersed us under water; but swinging back she lurched heavily to port, and again were we under water. Gradually the lurches decreased in extent, and after a few more rolls the masts continued stationary. " I had only my head above water, as I was supporting my wife; and I was afraid to elevate myself farther, as I knew that in that case the weight would be increased. Above me, on the mast, a sailor was perched, who called out in the most imploring accents to some persons in a boat to come and take the people off, for some time in vain. When the vessel ultimately sunk, the quarter-deck at the stern was clustered with human beings, like a beehive; and of these but few were saved, as the vortex absorbed them, and they were so numerous as to impede each other in their attempts to save themselves. " On the shrouds of the mizzen mast, near where we were, there were several persons clustered, three females hanging on by one rope. At this time the companion cover floated off, and three persons contrived to keep by it until they were rescued. After being about half an hour in the water, a shore boat came up, and was about to pick them up, I told the men to get a lady, who appeared much exhausted, my wife was taken in next, and, as quickly as possible, all supported by the mast were speedily rescued. The boat then went to the mainmast, and took off the captain and another man or two, and then proceeded to the shore, where we were met by a little girl, who said we must come to her mammy's house as they had a nice fire to warm us, and would make us comfortable. When I first came on deck before returning to dress, they were lowering the starboard quarter boat; but I was below when they accomplished the somewhat difficult feat, as the ropes had got entangled. On coming upon deck the second time, the Captain, who was in his drawers and shirt, said that if they all stuck to the ship there would be no danger. I accordingly went down and told the ladies so, which calmed them for a little, but as the water rose, and the lurch of the vessel increased, the alarm was soon renewed, and the ladies all rushed on deck. Into one of the boats some four or five men got in and rowed away in spite of the cries and entreaties of those on board the sinking ship. There appeared to be great difficulty in launching the boats as the tackles were all entangled; and when launched they were in danger of filling, as the plug-holes were all open, and no corks or plugs could be found, the result was that, although the passengers kept baling the boats with their hats, they were in danger of sinking before the boats reached the shore. Into one of the boats a number of gentlemen had crowded, when a cry got up that the ladies should be allowed in first ; and accordingly a number of the gentlemen did get out, and admit ladies ; but the boat had not left the vessel's side when she swamped; but, after being emptied she righted, and although half full of water, a number of others got into her, and I believe ultimately reached land. The McNeill's eldest daughter, although alive when she was brought ashore, soon died. She was a handsome, joyous, happy creature, and walked the deck till a late hour, in all the health and joyousness of youth. Alas! how soon was all changed; and ere a few hours elapsed she was a breathless corpse. Mrs. Merrilees of Liverpool had a little child about 9 months old in her arms. When she was overpowered with the waters, she sunk, and, on rising to the surface, her baby was dead, and floated away out of her arms. The mother was saved, and when she recovered a little, she was bewailing her sad bereavement when the body of the little innocent was brought into the house. The scene that ensued may be imagined. Mr. Tait, baker, of this city, swam on shore with his little boy on his back most of the way, and both were saved. The Rev. Mr. Peughe, the Episcopal' clergyman of Paisley, had a little child on board, about twelve years of age, who was under the charge of the stewardess. After the alarm was given, she proceeded to dress her little charge, and took her on deck, the poor little child exclaiming," I know you will not leave me."—" No, no, I never will," exclaimed the noble woman; but, alas, the remorseless surge claimed them as its own. Four instances came under my own observation where husbands and wives were saved through their mutual aid, in circumstances of awful peril and almost hopeless danger. " There were about 20 bodies recovered when we left, including Dr. Burns. Several of these were females, and three of them children. The females had little else on than their night-clothes, and some only their chemises. Nothing could exceed the kindness of the villagers to the wants of the survivors; their houses, their larders, their wardrobes—their all, were freely placed at our disposal.

Mr. Archibald of Alloa, who, along with his son, was a passenger on board, both of whom are among the number rescued, states that he was on deck at the time the vessel first struck; but, except himself, be thinks, everyone else of the cabin passengers was below, and the only reason for his not being so likewise was, that the ship was so crowded that he could not get a berth. The rock was struck when the vessel was going at full speed, and as he had at the time every opportunity for observation, he confidently expresses his opinion that the atmosphere was as clear as at the hour, namely, about one o'clock, might have been expected. 'Though perhaps not light, it was assuredly not dark, and he could see the land with distinctness, and without the least difficulty. After referring to the consternation which the occurrence occasioned, Mr. Archibald proceeded to describe the position in which he found himself amid the panic-stricken throng. His first object was to secure his boy, and along with him he succeeded in getting into a boat—the first, he thinks, which was lowered. When about eight people got into her, some person from above, on board the steamer, let go one of the ropes, and the boat immediately fell on the side, towards the stern, and filled with water. The other rope was then thrown down, and she canted over altogether, precipitating those who had seated themselves in her into the sea. He, however, succeeded in keeping himself and his son above the surface till some people seized him by the arms, and they were both pulled down. At this critical juncture there was providentially pitched over to them a cork fender, with a rope attached, of which he, his son, and two other gentlemen immediately laid hold. By this means the four succeeded in keeping themselves above the surface for a considerable period, and till a boat from the shore came and picked them up. They had considerable difficulty in getting into the boat, but in this the whole of the group at last succeeded, with the exception of an old gentleman, who in his endeavours to do so sank, and was drowned. On reaching the shore, Mr. Archibald was greatly exhausted, but he believes that they were landed before the steamer sunk.

## British North Daily Mail 20th June 1850

Sir—l enclose a letter which, I believe, will interest your readers. It is written to a cousin in London by schoolboy of 14, [Master Darrock] who, with his tutor was on his way home for the holidays. Mr. P. and I set sail from Liverpool on the 17th, at half past 3 in the afternoon. We had a beautiful smooth passage, all the ladies remaining on deck till late. At half-past 11, as we passed the Isle of Man, we both went down to bed. At about half past 1 in the morning I was awoken by hearing the other gentlemen getting up and talking, and from them I heard that we had run aground. I woke Mr. P. and he dressed quickly and ran upstairs. I in the meantime dressed very quietly, thinking there was no danger, as the sea was so calm and the shore near, and had just got on my trousers, boots, and shirt, when down came Mr. P. saying we had gone ashore off the Irish coast (which I thought rather curious), and that I had better come on deck. Just then, the vessel sinking lower, the water poured into the cabin in a torrent. We both rushed on deck accompanied by several ladies in their nightclothes. We were only about 300 yards from the shore when we struck. The land was quite visible and the light of Portpatrick. We both went to the stern, and Mr. P. from there went amidships, and I clung to the binnacle. The screams of the poor ladies, the prayers of the men, such as "Oh ! Lord help us !" God Save us !" and the roaring of the steam were frightful. Presently, the vessel heeled right over, till the deck was almost perpendicular. Then came the most frightful part of the scene; the poor women slid down under the lee-bulwarks, and were swept out by the next wave—their screams were heart-rending; just then the passengers launched the life -boat, but it was swamped instantaneously, and all drowned except two; the seamen were too much terrified to do anything, but some jumped overboard, and others ran up the shrouds. I in the meantime, was clinging to the binnacle (a part just before the wheel, where the compass is kept), and, when she went on her beam ends, I immediately divested myself of trousers and boots, and bung them overboard, knowing that I could not swim with them on. Having done that, I waited patiently for the result, crying to God for help, as also most of the passengers were, when I saw the steam coming up the companion, and heard it making a horrible bubbling noise. I thought that all was lost, and that we should have a precious blow up, so committing my life into the hands of God I plunged overboard. There were about six other men who jumped in with me, and they struck out so hard that they got me under the water for about a minute, however, I soon got up and struck boldly for my life. When I had swam about forty yards I came to a chest, on which a man was supporting himself I made for it, and reached it, but the seaman was in such an agony of terror that he knew not what he did, and in foolishly endeavouring to get to the top of the chest, he turned it round like a treadwheel. I could not shift my hands as quickly as he pulled it over, and so I was pushed right under the water for about two minutes. At that awful time I felt the water coming in my ears and nose, and thought on home and my parents, and felt that I should never see them more, I was giving up, but just then I felt new vigour in my limbs, and determined not to relinquish life without a struggle. I then dived down till I got free of the man and chest and swam to some things which were floating near, and got something like a desk under one arm and a kind of wooden grating under the other; with these I kept up a long while, but looking round I saw the large chest with the man, who had stopped pulling it over. I swam to it, therefore, and told the man not to pull it as our safety depended on it ; he remained quiet, but by way of precaution, I still kept the wooden grating under my other arm. Soon, another man joined us on the chest, he got on the end, and told us to strike out for the land, which we all did, and were getting on very well when we saw to our inexpressible joy a large boat come round the point out of Portpatrick ; we all set up a shout "Oh, save us!" "Oh, we are drowning," and all that kind of thing. Presently the boat heard us and approached, and you cannot tell the feelings which arose my breast. Then the man in the bow laid hold of me to pull me in, I was too weak to scramble in. As soon as he had laid me on the forecastle, I fell right over into the body of the boat, but then I was so cold I began to jump and cut away into the stern sheets, and I sat down shivering like a dozen drowned rats. The other two men were pulled in more dead than alive; they lay in the bottom of the boat quite exhausted. We went on and picked up a poor woman off a piece of wreck where she had been floating. Then we went to the wreck, which had gone down, I suppose, when I was under the chest; the water, then being low tide, was not up to her crosstrees, and there were a great many clinging to the shrouds. We took a woman and her baby and about eight men off the wreck, and then made for land. I all the time was jumping to keep myself warm, having nothing on but a shirt. When we got into the harbour I ran up the landing stairs. At the top there was an old woman with a shawl in her hand, which she cast about me, and took me to her master's house, whose name was Captain Hawes, R.N. They gave to us some warm brandy and water, put me into a warm bed, where I soon fell asleep. After Mr P left me he went to the companion, and when the Orion heeled over he cut up the shrouds, where he remained till the last boat; he was the last to quit the unfortunate vessel. When I woke I found him by my bedside. About six o'clock, they signalled the Fleetwood boat to come in, as she was passing at the time; she did so, but I had no clothes, but they borrowed some for me in the village —trousers that came down to my knees, a waistcoat that would not button, a grey coat all torn, a pair of boots a mile too high, and a Scotch bonnet; so with these elegant vestments you may imagine what a figure I was. I went on board the Fenella, and there found a large number of my fellow sufferers; some had no boots, some no coat, and we were altogether like a gang of gipsies. There were about six dead bodies on the shore when I left, and a boat came alongside the Fenella with a lady and two men quite dead; the lady had some seaweed on her face. The Fenella's captain charged us nothing, and at Troon we got into the train telling the news as we went. I got into the omnibus at Glasgow just missing Papa, who was at the Post-office, and created great sensation in the above-mentioned vehicle; one poor woman was so touched that she slipped a fourpenny piece into my hand, and was with great difficulty persuaded to take it back. When I got home, I told mamma that the Orion was aground, not to alarm her, and she was so glad to see me that she never noticed my dress, but when she went into the dining room she told them, laughing, that looked like a shipwrecked mariner. Papa soon came home and told her, and she was most awfully frightened when she heard the dangers I had escaped. Captain McNeill of Colonsay was drowned, with his wife and two daughters; his two sons were saved. It all happened through the carelessness of the captain's running too near shore.

## North British Daily Mail 22nd June 1850.

Captain McKechnie of Greenock, and his lady, were among the passengers, and we are glad to say were saved. This result, they owe, under Providence, to the coolness of Mr. McKechnie. Awakened by the striking of the vessel, they sprang out of their berths, and they reached the deck almost undressed, and he at once saw their danger. He thought be saw how he might save his own life had he but his wife to look to, but how his wife was to be preserved he could not see. She urged him to look to himself, she would await her fate. This he refused to do, and encouraging her, he desired her to attend to no directions but his and both might yet be saved. Soon after he found part of a hatch covering, and placed Mrs McKechnie upon it, imploring her to attend implicitly to his directions alone, and to hold on by him. The ship now gradually settling, and as she sunk he seized the lanyards of the mizzen mast, which passed through his hands as the ship sank, the hatch floating, and Mrs McKechnie having hold of her husband. On the Orion reaching the bottom, Mr McKechnie saw the probability of their being saved greatly increased. He also caught hold of two ladies floating past, whom he also placed on the hatch, and thus providentially preserved. Boats were now leaving the shore; and his only fear now was lest his charge should be overpowered by the sight of the poor struggling people sinking around. His efforts were, however, crowned with success, and they arrived at Greenock on Wednesday, by the Princess Royal. Sometime after landing, the worthy individual was met by a gentleman, who, warmly grasping his hand, exclaimed, " Sir, you saved any life." The captain did not seem aware what particular individuals had benefitted by his praiseworthy exertions; but he modestly expressed his gratitude that he had been of some little service to any of his fellow passengers.

## Dundee Perth and Couper Advertiser
*Adam Forbes*


I was steerage passenger by the Orion. The hour advertised for the sailing of the vessel was three o'clock P.M.; but we did not get away till about four. was beautiful evening; there was no wind, and the sea was perfectly calm, and as smooth as glass. I remained on deck till about half-past nine or ten o'clock, when I went below in the steerage. The vessel was then a long way past the Isle of Man, and the land was not visible. All were cheerful below and singing and merriment was going on. I remained below till about one o'clock, when I returned to the deck, and found the vessel just passing a point that runs out into the sea, called the Mull of Galloway. We seemed to be then about a mile from land and I could see it distinctly. A good many passengers were on deck. Several women and children were lying about the funnel and in other sheltered places. The air was not cold. The cabin passengers seemed to be all below in their berths. The only individuals the crew I saw on deck were the second mate, the steersman, and the look-out, walking on the gangway. have heard it said there were two walking there, but I saw only one. Nothing occurred to attract my notice, and I went below, after being about twenty minutes on deck. I understand that, at this time, the vessel was making about 15 knots an hour. Before going down, I observed that were much closer to the land than when I came up. The vessel was then nearing the point at Portpatrick. We might have been about half a mile, or three-quarters of mile from the land, when I went down. We were bearing towards the point or promontory. It was then quite clear around the vessel, that is to say, there was no fog. There was a thick gathered mist on the top of the rising ground beyond Portpatrick, but in the low parts and down at the level of the coast one could see quite distinctly as in a clear night. The daylight was faintly breaking through to the east, and you could distinguish the vessel from end to end. The stars were not visible, but still the night, or rather the morning, was an ordinary clear one, and daylight was breaking beautifully, and the vessel was going as steadily as possible. Two other steerage passengers went down along with me, and we found those below, of whom there were good number, men, women, and children, employed as before, some lying asleep, others laughing and singing. I went and got a seat on the starboard side, that is to say, on the side next the land, where I sat down, and was listening about ten minutes to the singing, and was laughing at the jokes, when crash took place which I could compare to nothing but a peal of thunder. I kept seat for a few seconds after the crash, thinking it impossible the vessel could have gone upon a rock. I thought something had gone wrong with the engine, the crash was so like a heavy fall of machinery. The other passengers began to rush to the hatchway, and I started to my feet. The water poured into the steerage from the land side, having struck the rock on that side where I was sitting. I then made the best of way to get on deck but was among the last to get up the hatchway. When I got on deck I hurried to the bow of the vessel to see what was wrong. The steam was then going off through the steam-pipe with a fearful noise. It was let off intentionally. I looked from the bow and saw the land quite near and very distinct. I think I could have thrown a stone to the land. Could have discerned a moving object, such as a man, on the land very distinctly. Daylight was not much more visible than when I had been last on deck, but it was quite clear for that time of the morning, and the sea perfectly smooth. The vessel was then lying with her side obliquely to the shore, but I observed that she was gradually veering round with her head towards the shore. I observed also that she was rapidly settling down by the head, where I was standing- I then hurried to the quarter deck, where the boats were. We met the cabin passengers rushing forward along the deck, with nothing but their night-dresses. The general cry was, is there danger?" I observed the captain among the rest, in his shirt and drawers. He was standing near the engine-house, shouting out that there was no danger, and to keep calm. I understood his impression at the time to be, that she had settled on the rock, and that there was really no danger of the vessel going down. The side of the vessel where she had struck—namely, that next the land — was then gradually sinking, and the bow was down almost under the water, and still sinking deeper. At that time I was standing at the quarterdeck, the lower side of the vessel, next the land. One of the boats was suspended there on the outside. A great crowd of cabin and steerage passengers, including many ladies and several children, were collected there. Two or three of the crew were among them. All were attempting to get into the boat, which was still hanging at the side the vessel. I got into it, with ten or eleven others, of whom one was a lady. The screaming on board the vessel at that time was terrific. The crew seemed to make no systematic attempt to keep back the passengers and to lower the boats. One boat was hanging on each side of the quarter deck, and another two were lying behind the paddle boxes. There were four boats in all. The last mentioned two were completely covered over with canvas, and each of them was lashed down three different places. They were completely covered up and seemed more for show than use. Only one these was ever got unfastened—the other went down with the ship. It is not true that the boats of the ship did much service. Most of the lives were saved by boats from Portpatrick. When got into the boat on the starboard side of the quarter-deck, along with other ten eleven persons, those on deck commenced to lower it down. The stern rope would not run, and only the bow of the boat went down. The passengers in the vessel then made the bow-rope fast, and the stern rope was still fast. The boat was at that time hanging almost perpendicular, with the bow pointing to the water. We were clinging to the seats to prevent ourselves falling into the water. There was then a cry from some of those along with me and the boats to cut the ropes, and one of the persons in the boat got out his knife and cut the bow rope. The boat then fell down perpendicular, hanging stern upwards, with the bow partly in the sea. About a quarter of the length of the boat was under water. We were almost all pitched into the sea immediately. I was thrown right into the water, but got hold the boat again, and held fast by one of the seats. I was all in the water except my head. There were one or two above me, hanging by the seats of the boat, and several round about in the water, some clinging, and others sinking to rise no more. There was then a cry from the ship above to cut the stern rope, which some person on board the ship did. With the weight of us who were clinging, and the bow of the boat pointing down under water, the boat immediately plunged down, filled, capsized, and floated keel upwards. I went under water with her as well as several others, and when rose again to the surface, I saw the bottom of the boat upwards, and got hold of her keel. I can swim, and the sea was so smooth that I would have made an attempt to swim ashore, but so many women and children were floating and struggling about, that I was afraid to strike out. I did make the attempt, but was immediately caught by both arms, and struggled with difficulty back again to the boat, to which there were four or five others clinging. The steamer was then rapidly going down. She was down almost to the paddle boxes, and great numbers were throwing themselves into the sea to endeavour to float ashore. Some ropes were then thrown over from the ship's side, which people were lowering themselves into the sea. I got hold of one of these ropes, along with three others—one woman and two men, all clung to this rope, and held on for the space of four or five minutes. then saw the other quarter boat, from the opposite side, making away to the land, with only thirteen or fourteen persons in it. We screamed and shouted out to them to come to our assistance and take us off. The boat would have held twenty thirty more, but the persons in it paid no attention to us and made for the shore. I understand there were two or three firemen belonging to the ship in it. This was the first boat that landed passengers from the ship. Up to that time there was no other boat in use. I then looked to the land, when I saw boat coming from Portpatrick, which was about a quarter of a mile off, rather back from where we struck. This boat was rowed by two young men belonging to Portpatrick. On nearing the ship it went first to the stern and picked up a man who was holding on by the helm. It then picked up woman in the water and came round to us. We were quite close to the stern. They picked four of us off that rope. They were almost going away without us so many others were grappling to get hold of the boat, everyone entreating to be saved in the most piteous manner. Fortunately, they stopped and pulled us in, however. If had been five minutes longer at the rope I would have been obliged to let go my arms and whole body were so benumbed with cold. We then made for the shore. The boat was a very small one and was completely laden with seven or eight persons. We were safely landed Portpatrick. In proceeding to the shore, we saw three or four boats coming out to the ship. When we left the ship, she was almost under water to the funnel, and the screaming was perfectly harrowing. A great number were then on deck, several clinging to the rigging, and many floating about the ship in all directions, some of whom were holding on by pieces of wood and other articles. I heard some say that the captain opposed the boats being lowered at all, and called on all to remain in the ship, saying that there was no danger, threatening to cut off the hands of the first man who should touch the boats.

## Glasgow Herald, June 21st 1850

John Cameron, commercial traveller with Messrs. Clapperton & Co: "1 went aboard the Orion, at Liverpool, with Mr Marchbank, also of Messrs.

Clapperton's house. It was a beautiful afternoon, and we spent it pleasantly on board in the company with Mr. Archibald, of Alloa, and Mr. John Hume, wool merchant, now lost. The steamer was excessively crowded with passengers, a large number of them being ladies. Every berth was occupied, as well as the seats and sofas. I walked the deck with Mr. Archibald until, think, about 1 o clock in the morning, when I went down to my berth on one of the sofas in the saloon. The weather was then fine, and, indeed, it could not be said to be dark during the whole night. I threw off only my coat and boots and laid down on the cushion, amongst the others, and immediately above the sofa where Mr Marchbank was asleep. I think about twenty minutes after I went down and before I fell asleep I felt the vessel grate along her side or bottom as if she was being ripped up with a saw and at the same time the engine stopped. I lay there for a minute thinking what could this mean as I had no notion the Orion was going to stop before Greenock. A number of gentlemen who had been sleeping but up their heads on finding the shock and sprung out of their berths and ran up on deck in their shirts. Up to this time there was no intimation from the deck that there was anything wrong. I then also got up and pulled on my boots and at the same time awoke Mr Marchbank telling him to get up as I feared something was wrong. Hurrying on my coat and great coat I went on deck with Mr Marchbank in the act of rising to follow me, or so I understood. On going up the stair I met the passengers running down again, I went on without remark. There was great confusion on deck with a great many people gathered at the side nearest the land. I heard someone cry, "Lower the boats, she is sinking.' From the numbers gathered at that side I thought any boat lowered there might be swamped so I went to the larboard side. There were few people round the who I think were mostly firemen and engineers with just one crewman belonging to the Orion, who were crying for assistance to lower the boat. I said if he lowered one side, I would lower the other. At this time the ship was visibly sinking in the water; the stern was canting up, and the sparks from funnel were rushing up like from a house on fire. We lowered the boat until she was level with the bulwarks of the ship, when a considerable number - I think about dozen men—scrambled into her. I then leapt in myself, still holding the rope and lowering away at the same time. When got down the sea, which was quite smooth, the sailor swung down with the other rope. The boat was entangled, however with something like broad belts, which I cut with my knife and then she floated clear of the ship. We had no oars however, and when we called out for them a pair was thrown by a passenger, who I think was Mr Kidston. We then discovered that the boat was making water rapidly as the plug had not been put in; but a sailor passenger from Liverpool, got a handkerchief and partially stopped the hole with it. We then moved round the stern towards the Lighthouse pier, which was not far and doing we saw that the other stern boat had swamped, and that several people were floating in the water. Some of our people proposed to take them in, others objected saying. They would drown us also boat would be back immediately and render assistance. There were fourteen, I think, in our boat. I sat holding the handkerchief in the plughole the greater part of the way; I don't know who rowed or had charge of the boat. When we were about halfway, I saw the ship lurch and settle down, disappearing all but the funnel and the masts; and at this time the most heart screams proceeded from her, both from male and female voices. We landed, and the two sailors immediately went back to render help. When we reached the pier, the boats belonging to the inhabitants of Portpatrick were pushing fast out to the wreck. I stood at the bottom of stairs leading to the pier-head and handed up passengers who were landed at this point. They of both men and women, and almost all in deplorable condition. Miss McNeill, of Collonsay, a tall young lady of 19 years of age, was one of them. She walked the pier stairs unaided, but I learnt that she died immediately after. Many of these rescued especially the ladies, who were conscious, were in a terrible state of dreadful agony regarding the fate of their relations some of whom were saved by other boats, and others perished. I was engaged in this way till they began to land the passengers at another spot nearer the houses. I went there and remained till the captain, who was the last came out, and I helped him to land. He had nothing but shirt and trousers, I stripped and lent him coat. I never saw my friend Mr Marchbank again in but his body was brought ashore at 8 o'clock. He had remained to dress himself, not having his clothes and I suspect that this delay was the cause of his not being able escape. My conviction is that many may have be drowned in their berths, she went down so rapidly, the danger so great, that all who reached the deck may have been taken up in the effort to save themselves, without giving notice to those who might be below. The number of passengers was very great and I heard the captain say during the morning that there were 172 cabin passengers, and 50 in the steerage the humane conduct of the inhabitants of Portpatrick is beyond all praise. I left with the Princess Royal for Glasgow at 4 o'clock Wednesday.

# References

## Chapter Three
1 and 3 - The Scotsman 22nd June 1850

1 and 3 - The Scotsman 22nd June 1850

2 – Bolton Chronicle June 29th 1850: The Art of Swimming. To the Editor of the Bolton Chronicle. Sir, Being much interested in the particulars of the wreck of The Orion, from having frequently been a passenger from Glasgow to Liverpool and vice versa, I have read with interest the account of the narrow escapes by swimming and floating upon pieces of timber; but no case has pleased me more than that of a young lady, who, in the excitement of the moment, remembered that she had heard that if person would lie on his back and move the hands gently they would float for long time, and who therefore did so, and was saved. Had many of the drowned done so, they, too, would have been saved. It cannot be too much impressed upon the minds of young and old, that the position above described is a certain means prolonging life for many hours, if the sea is ordinarily calm. Visiting Blackpool lately, I was surprised to see out of many hundreds who bathed, not one swimmer but myself. It is a shame for any Bolton person having the advantage of the public baths, to be unable to participate in the pleasure, and, in the case of many in The Orion, the salvation that useful accomplishment procures. Hoping this notice may cause many to learn to swim, I am, &c., Bolton, June 26th. A Swimmer.

## Chapter Four
1 – Techniques adopted by the Society for the Recovery of Drowned Persons included warming the victim, removing swallowed or inhaled water by ensuring the head was in a position lower than the feet, applying manual pressure to the abdomen, releasing air into the victims mouth either by mouth to mouth or bellows, tickling the victims throat, and stimulating the victim by means of either an oral or rectal fumigation with tobacco smoke, bellows were used to drive tobacco smoke, a known irritant, into the intestines through the anus and finally bloodletting. History of Cardiopulmonary Resuscitation, Wikipedia.org. The chest pressure arm life method was not introduced until 1858 by a London physician called Dr Silvester. Cpr.heart.org

## Chapter Five
1 – Coleraine Chronicle 3rd August 1850

## Chapter Six
1 – The Letter from Lawrence Banner read:
Ladies and Gentlemen, —The bearer of this account of the late calamitous loss of life, was cabin passenger on board the ' Orion," at the time of the disaster his name being Mr. Banner, of Montreal, Canada, North America, he only arrived the week previous per packet ship, Wisconsin, via, New York, at Liverpool, and was in the employ as buyer, for the respectable firm of Strang, and Co., of Montreal, dry goods merchants, of that city, whose employ he has been during the last ten years; he had in his possession in a belt around his body the sum £1,000 in gold, partly the property of his employers, which got unbuckled during his exertions to save two young ladies, passengers, whom he landed in safety. but had the misfortune lose the gold, which went to the bottom, as also did his portmanteaux containing his clothing, letters of credit, introductions, instructions, and being now left penniless in strange country, 2,500 miles from his native land, until he be put possession of advice from the firm in America. He would therefore beg most respectfully to submit this account the noble ship, trusting to the sympathising feelings the British public, particularly for support which his case warrants, and hopes commercial friends and ladies and gentlemen may find it convenient to read and purchase this narrative, being left to their own generosity as to price.—And oblige, ladies and gentlemen, your bumble and obedient servant, "LAWRENCE BANNER." W. Campbell and Co., of Glasgow, and the captain of the Orion said they were forgeries. He was condemned to hard labour for a month.

## Chapter Seven
1) This is not a full account of the trial, it is drawn from newspaper articles and the report in the book by John Shaw. Further details of the charges and the trial can be seen at archive.org - Shaw, John. Reports of Cases Before the High Court and Circuit Courts of Justiciary in Scotland during the years 1848 to 1852.T & T Clark, Edinburgh 1853

## The Portpatrick Boatmen

Daniel and William Alexander
Hugh Alexander senior and Hugh Junior
Allen Auld
James Adair
James and John Crawford
James Davidson
James Jess
Andrew McDowell
Thomas McMicken
John McCarlie
William Puffel
William Wallace
Mr Robertson surgeon of Portpatrick
As listed in Rev Joseph Clarke's The Wreck of the Orion
To which should be added William Oke and Captain Edward Hawes.

## Passengers

Further information about some of the passengers on board the Orion.

Mr and Mrs Hurst of Hamar Hall, Rochdale. Lost a son and servant girl. The family were taking the Orion in a party with Mrs Whitehead of Saddleworth and her daughters Mary and Hannah to join the Admiral about to sail to Melbourne. The Whiteheads had been travelling to join two of Mrs Whitehead's sons who had been living in Australia for more than ten years. Mr Hurst managed to save himself along with three others by clinging to a box. While keeping a secure grasp with both hands he made a desperate effort to save his son by holding him with his teeth, but he soon became exhausted and lost hold when the poor boy went down.

Dr Nicol of Littleton near Girvan along with his wife and three children, two boys and a girl. One of the daughters perished.

Captain Alexander McNeill, Laird of Colonsay, Oronsay, Ardlussa and Gigha age 59 and his wife Anne Elizabeth, formerly Carstairs, daughter and co heiress of John Carstairs, age 47. Their daughter Cecil Anne, age 17, and Hester Mary, age six. Captain McNeill had served with the 21st Argyll and Sutherland Highlanders in the Peninsula War 1808 to 14. Their two teenage sons, John 14 and Alexander 16 swam to shore. The Captain was the brother of the Lord Advocate of Scotland. John Carstairs McNeill was given a scholarship to Addiscombe "in consideration of his sad bereavement" by the chairman of the East India Company, Mr J Shepherd. He later became a highly decorated soldier gaining a Victoria Cross during the New Zealand wars. He was educated at Addiscombe and St Andrews. He was knighted and in retirement became an equerry to Queen Victoria. Alexander McNeill served with the Royal Engineers during the Indian Rebellion of 1857. He later joined his brother in New Zealand where they bought and named Ardlussa Station, after the family estate on Jura.

Mrs Smith, recently widowed mother of nine children who was travelling to Glasgow from Montreal to visit relatives with her brother in law Mr Scott, his wife and daughter. The Scott family had been living in Canada but intended setting in Scotland. The party had been joined in Liverpool by a young relative, Miss Jameson who was returning to her parents in Glasgow. All drowned except for Miss Jameson

Mr Thomas Kidston, son of Bailie John Kidstone of Stirling had been in America and had returned by the Europa on his way home from Liverpool. He threw himself into the sea and managed to reach land safely.

Mr John Roby, formerly a partner in the banking house of Messrs Fenton and Roby of Rochdale. He had been retired for some years and was on his way to Edinburgh with his wife and daughter, where they intended to live for some time. His wife and daughter were amongst the saved. His body was found the same day and conveyed to Rochdale for burial. Mr Roby was a highly accomplished author of several books including Traditions of Lancashire, Tour on the Continent and volumes of poetry. He was 58 years old and related to Rev Wm Roby of Manchester and brother-in-law of the late Rev John Ely of Leeds.

Dr Burns, Professor of Surgery at the University of Glasgow. Eldest surviving son of the late Rev Dr Burns of Barony Parish, Glasgow (known as the Father of the Church of Scotland). He had been appointed to the chair of surgery at the University in 1815 and was revered across Europe. His eldest son was a major in the army.

### Passengers Interred at Portpatrick old church yard.

Robert Haslam and William Latham

Travelling with their friend Johnathon Settle, Robert Haslam had been going to Glasgow to consult the eminent surgeon Dr Burns, not realising that the doctor was also on board the Orion. William Latham and Robert Haslam are commemorated in Portpatrick churchyard where Mr Latham was laid to rest.

A memorial states: This tablet has been contributed by the members of the Loyal Orthodox Lodge of the Independent Order of Oddfellows, Bolton Le Moor of the Manchester Unity in testimony of their profound regret for the loss of William Latham PPGM and Robert Haslam, Treasurer of the above lodge who are interred here.

Robert Haslam, 35, Yeoman of Bolton Le Moor. He was a man of strict probity and sterling honesty, affable and good natured and a worthy brother and one who wished to leave the world a better place than he found it. William Latham, 48, Laid by his brother Peter Latham. His genius and inflexible integrity procured for him approbation and affection of all who knew him. He left a wife and four children.

Thomas Gladstone – ten year old son of Laurence Gladstone, great nephew of the politician and British Prime Minister, William Ewart Gladstone.

Francis McMurry age 21

Robert Trail of Montrose age 30.

Margaret Gardner, beloved daughter of John Nicol MD of Liverpool, age 9 years and two months.

The Splatt family.

John and Betsy Splatt and their four adult daughters were on their way from their home in Devon to Glasgow to join the ship the Admiral to travel to Australia. Their elder son William had emigrated in 1840, with two brothers, becoming a successful merchant, sheep farmer and member of the legislative council of Victoria. He was joined the following year by his elder sister and her family. They had been trying to persuade their parents and sisters to join them there, believing the chances of the four girls finding husbands would be better in the colony. John had been a Yeoman farmer born in 1780, farming at Powderham. He had married his first wife Fanny Stokes in 1805 giving birth to a daughter, given the same name, the following year. When his wife died John moved to Chudleigh and took over Northwood Farm where he met a young widow, Elizabeth whom he married in 1810. William, the eldest of their ten children together, was born in 1811 when they moved again to Willsworthy Farm in Kenton. After the loss of his wife and four daughters on the Orion, John returned to Devon and settled in a home he called Melbourne House in Heavitree, Exeter. He died in 1859 and is buried at Kenton churchyard. William Francis Splatt, returned from Australia in 1854 a very wealthy man and later became the first mayor of Torquay. He erected a memorial stone to his mother and four sisters at Chudleigh Church. On it he described his mother as "blessed with a gentle disposition, she was deservedly beloved by all who knew her and most tenderly endeared her to their children, six of them lament their irreparable loss." The gravestone at Portpatrick remembers Betsy Splatt, wife, 68, Mary Ann, 38, Elizabeth, 31, Susanna, 27 and Anna Maria, 22.

*Gravestone in Portpatrick Old Churchyard erected by John Splatt*
*in memory of his wife and four daughters.*

## The Orion's Crew    wages

T Henderson Master    £4

G Langlands First Mate  £2

R Wilson Clyde Pilot    £1/10 (pounds and shillings)

J Williams Second Mate £1/10

R Walker Carpenter        £1/8

E Jones Cook        £1

T Miller Cook's boy    20 shillings

G Williamson Seaman      £1/1

J Kerr Seaman    £1/1

C Nailie Seaman      £1/1

J Donald Seaman      £1/1

D Walker Seaman      £1/1

D Campbell Seaman      £1/1

J Kelly Seaman    £1/1

J Stewart Seaman      £1/1

J Aird Seaman    £1/1

C McHeacham Apprentice        7 shillings

P Harrisay Apprentice    7 shillings

J Dunn Apprentice    7 shillings

A Crocket engineer not aboard

J Pattison second engineer      £1/15

J Livingston fireman    £1/1

Ten further crew comprising a principal and three other stewards, a stewardess, firemen and coal trimmers.

Details from the National Records of Scotland

## Newspaper sources

Aberdeen Herald and General Advertiser

Ayr Advertiser

Belfast Newsletter

Bolton Chronicle

Bristol Times and Mirror

Caledonian Mercury

Chelmsford Chronicle

Cheltenham Chronicle

Coleraine Chronicle

Cork Examiner

Derry Journal

Dover Telegraph and Cinque Ports General

Dumfries and Galloway Standard
Dundee Courier
Dundee, Perth and Cupar Advertiser
The Era
Exeter and Plymouth Gazette
Gallovidian
Glasgow Gazette
Glasgow Herald
Greenock Advertiser
Inverness Courier
Kendal Mercury
Limerick Chronicle
Liverpool Journal
Liverpool Mercury
Liverpool Standard and General Commercial Advertiser
Liverpool Times
London Evening Mail
London Illustrated News
Lloyd's List
Manchester Guardian
Monmouthshire Beacon
North and South Shields Gazette and Northumberland and Durham Advertiser
Newcastle Courant
North British Daily Mail
Perthshire Constitutional
Perthshire Advertiser
Reformers Gazette
Shipping and Mercantile Gazette
The Scotsman
Sirling Observer
Westmoreland Gazette
Wigtownshire Free Press
Wiltshire and Gloucestershire Standard

## Websites
Archive.org
Britishnewspaperarchive.co.uk
Canmore.org
Chudleighhistorygroup.co.uk
Clydeships.co.uk

Dustydocs.com
Futuremuseum.co.uk
Glasgowstory.com
Gracesguide.co.uk
Historyanswers.co.uk
Historic-uk.com
Liverpoolnauticalresearchsociety.org
Oldmerseytimes.co.uk
Portpatrickchurchyard.org.uk
Theanchorline.co.uk
Universitystory.gla.ac.uk
Wikipedia
Wrecksite.eu

## Bibliography
Bodey, Gordon 4th March 2010 Liverpool Nautical Research Society
Clarke, Rev Joseph M A, The Wreck of the Orion. Longman, Brown, Green and Longman. Manchester. 1851
Cunningham R R. Portpatrick Through the Ages.
Hocking, Charles. Dictionary of Disasters During the Age of Steam.
Kennedy, John. History of Steam Navigation, Kessinger Publishing. 2007
MacHaffie, Fraser G. Portpatrick to Donaghadee. Stranraer and District Local History Trust 2001
Miller, Peter C. Galloway Shipwrecks. Sunquest. 1992
Moir Peter and Crawford, Ian Clyde Shipwrecks, 1997
Maenpaa, Sari. The Origins of Women's Employment on British Passenger Liners 1850 to 1940. Tandfonline.com
National Records of Scotland, Lord Advocate's Department: Misc Papers.
Robins, Nick. Scotland and the Sea: The Scottish Dimension in Maritime History.
Shaw, John. Reports of Cases Before the High Court and Circuit Courts of Justiciary in Scotland during the years 1848 to 1852.T & T Clark, Edinburgh 1853

In April 1977 the position of the wreck of the Orion was reported as 54 50 34N, 005 07 22W with remains lying on a gravel bottom dotted with an odd rocky outcrop. Most of the remains were buried in gravel. The site was less than 95 metres offshore. The published harbour plan notes Orion Rock rising to 0.6m depth from a rocky seabed in a general depth of between about 2 and 5m about 220m NW of the ruined pierhead to the NW of Portpatrick harbour entrance. The wreck itself is not indicated. Information from RCAHMS (RJCM), 18 July 2003. Canmore.org.

Timber salvaged from the Orion went to make numerous pieces of furniture in Portpatrick – one of these, a chair, can be found in the museum at Stranraer. Little, if anything, now remains of the wreck. Author and diver Peter Miller reports that the original teams were clearly very efficient at salvaging the site. Some coins of little value were found by modern divers, one is now in my possession after coming up on an internet auction site. Unfortunately, as I was carrying out the research for this book the COVID-19 pandemic began making it impossible for me to carry out the further investigations I had planned. I did, however, manage to complete enough research to publish a first edition in time to mark the 170th anniversary of the wrecking, on the 18th June 2020. I would be interested to hear from anyone with relics from the Orion, families connected to the disaster or from anyone who has dived to the wreck. I can be contacted through Foggie Toddle Books in Wigtown.

## Thank you

I would like to thank Ruth Anderson QC, Anne Dunford, Kriss Nichol, Caroline Smith and Pauline Paterson for their help in producing this book.

## The Author

Jayne Baldwin is a writer, publisher and bookseller based in Wigtown, Scotland's National Book Town. She is the author of four books for children and two non-fiction books for adults, the Final Flight of Elsie Mackay and Mary Timney, Road to the Gallows.